POEMS OF FRANÇOIS VILLON

POEMS
of
François Villon
Including "*The Testament*"

Translated in the original verse forms by
NORMAN CAMERON

A Harbinger Book
Harcourt, Brace & World, Inc., New York

Library of Congress Catalog Card Number: 66-26471
First American Edition
Printed in the United States of America

CONTENTS

TRANSLATOR'S FOREWORD

MY qualifications for the task of translating Villon's poems into English verse lie in whatever gifts I may possess as a poet. I am not a medievalist nor a great scholar of the French language. In compiling the notes accompanying the translation, I have, in the main, taken material only from the four following sources, and mostly from the first-named:

L.T. *François Villon, Œuvres, Édition critique avec notices et glossaire, par Louis Thuasne. Paris, August Picard, Editeur,* 1923. This magnificent, three-volume work, of vast scholarship, also incorporates the results of research by previous scholars. Its notes and glossary are indispensable to any person, especially any non-French person, who wishes to gain the fullest possible understanding of Villon's poems.

G.P. *Villon, par Gaston Paris, de l'Académie Française, Librairie Hachette.* Divided into two sections, Life and Work, this book, written in 1900-1, gives a conspective and learned account of both.

A.L. *Étude Biographique sur François Villon, d'après les documents inédits conservés aux archives nationales, par Auguste Longnon, Paris, Henri Menu, Librairie-Éditeur, MDCCCLXXVII.* This work of pioneering research elucidated many previously perplexing questions.

7

C.M.   *François Villon, by Cecily Mackworth, with*
an introduction by Denis Saurat. Westhouse,
London, 1947. This book can be recom-
mended to English-speaking readers as giv-
ing a concise account of Villon's life, with
much interesting background information.

The initials above are those by which the sources are
referred to in the notes (which are usually not quotations
but condensations). Often the material I have used is
supplied by more than one of these sources; in which
cases I have usually referred to the work in which I first
found it.

The French text used is that edited by M. Thuasne;
but I have re-arranged the poems into an approximate
chronological order (except the ballades incorporated by
Villon in *The Testament,* some of which were probably
written earlier).

I have endeavoured to translate Villon's fifteenth-cen-
tury French into seventeenth-century English, to which
it corresponds in maturity, richness and resemblance to
the modern tongue. But I have used modern spelling
and punctuation.

Wherever possible, I have anglicized the Christian
names. Surnames and other proper names should be
pronounced, in accordance with the old practice, *anglice*:
e.g. Raguier as 'Ragwire' (with the stress on the second
syllable) and Dijon to rhyme with 'pigeon'.

Whilst adhering, except in two passages, to the original
verse-forms, I have given myself latitude in the use of
near-rhymes, which Villon very seldom uses. I plead as
justification that near-rhymes were familiar to English
readers in the seventeenth century and earlier. Sir
Thomas Wyatt (1503-42) rhymes, for example, harbour,

banner, suffer and displeasure. I have very seldom used the old French *rime riche* – that is to say, the rhyming of two words of different meanings but spelt exactly the same.

This is not a translation of Villon's complete works. I have omitted a few poems which seem to me either tedious or impossible to translate into rhyming verse with any degree of faithfulness to the original; and I have not attempted the utterly impossible task of translating into verse the ballades in Jargon, or Thieves' Cant.[1]

J. N. C.

BIOGRAPHICAL NOTE

THE poet was born at Paris, in the summer of 1431, of poor parents named Montcorbier, or de Montcorbier, after the village in the Bourbonnais from which they had recently come to the capital; or des Loges, after a smallholding near this village. His father died when he was a small boy, and the widow and son were left in poverty aggravated by the fact that Paris was suffering from English occupation, civil war and famine.

Some time between 1438 and 1440 François de Montcorbier, or des Loges, was taken under the care of Maître Guillaume de Villon, a chaplain of the church of Saint-Benoît-le-Bientourné, and went to live in the latter's house in the church's cloister. At the age of eleven he became a student in the Faculty of Arts of the University. In March 1449 he was received into the baccalaureate, and in August 1452 he became a Master of Arts – that is to say, a junior member of the clergy. About this time he fell into bad company (two of his friends, Colin des Cayeulx and Regnier de Montigny, were later hanged), neglected his studies and, according to legend, became famous for his skill in dishonestly obtaining free food and wine. It may have been at this time, too, that he conceived an unrequited passion, which was to endure for many years, for Katherine de Vausselles, who is thought to have been a niece and housemate of a canon of Saint-Benoît, and therefore François's near neighbour.

The poet's first known clash with the authorities occurred in June 1455, when he killed a priest in a brawl. On his deathbed the priest publicly forgave him, with the result that François, who had fled from Paris,

received royal pardon. (He had made two separate peti-
tions for pardon: one, to the chancery of the Great Seal,
signed 'maistre François des Loges autrement dit de
Villon', and the other, to the chancery of the Little Seal,
signed 'François de Montcorbier', and was pardoned under
both names.)

In October 1455, during this first exile of the poet
from Paris, letters of pardon were also issued to a certain
'Jehan des Loges, pedlar, a young person aged nineteen
years or thereabouts, a native of Anjou', further described
as 'a cleric', who was pardoned in respect of two thefts.
This 'young person' may have been the poet. If so, he
presumably understated his age in order to win clemency.
In *The Testament* (or *The Great Testament*) Villon
describes himself as a pedlar, and it may have been at this
time that he first fell in with the Coquille, a secret society
of criminals whose members often used peddling as a
cloak for a life of crime.

Early in 1456 Villon returned to Paris, to the house of
his foster-father, whose surname he from now on took as
his own, and in December of that year he wrote *The
Bequests* (or *The Little Testament*). At just about this
time, Villon and Colin de Cayeulx, together with an ex-
pert picklock named Petit Jean, a monk from Picardy
named Dom Nicolas, and a minor accomplice named Guy
Tabarie, broke into the College of Navarre, an institution
of the Faculty of Theology, and stole 500 gold crowns
from a safe. In May 1457 Tabarie got drunk in the
company of a prior of Paray who was visiting Paris, and
boasted of his skill as a thief. The prior reported the
matter to the authorities at the Châtelet prison, and on
their instructions set out to win the confidence of Tabarie
and his accomplices. Tabarie told the prior the story of
the robbery from the College of Navarre, and also told

him that Maître François Villon had gone to Angers to plan a robbery from a monk of that town who was Villon's maternal uncle. In June 1458 Tabarie was arrested and questioned under torture, and made a full confession.

Whether Villon had, in fact, meanwhile gone to Angers is not certain. If he had, he may have done so either from the motive ascribed to him by Tabarie, or simply to sponge on his uncle, or possibly to try to win the favour of the poet King René of Sicily, whose court was temporarily in that region, or from a combination of two or all of these motives. Wherever he was in 1457, he was not in Paris, and he must have learnt that he could not safely return there. He set out on a life of vagabondage, in the course of which he visited Moulins, residence of Duke John II of Bourbon, from whom he received a sum of money, and Blois, where for a short time he received hospitality and a stipend from the poet Duke Charles of Orleans. He apparently also tried, without success, to obtain help from the Archbishop of Bourges.

Between his visits to these great men, Villon presumably increased his acquaintance with the Coquille. In the summer of 1460 he was in prison at Orleans – for what crime it is not known – and apparently under sentence of death. In July, however, he was granted an amnesty on the occasion of an official visit to the city by Duke Charles. In the summer and autumn of 1461 he was again in prison and again under sentence of death – this time at Meung, his crime having been, according to local tradition, a robbery from a village church. In this prison he wrote two of his most famous ballades. Again he was granted an amnesty, in October, the occasion this time being a visit to Meung by Louis XI, who had recently succeeded to the throne.

Late in 1461 Villon wrote *The Testament* (or *The Great Testament*). M. Thuasne thinks that he had by this time returned to Paris. M. Gaston Paris and Miss Mackworth, however, infer from internal evidence of the poem that he had not yet done so. In any case, he was in Paris shortly afterwards. About this time he wrote a number of ballades in Jargon, or Thieves' Cant. In November 1462 he was in the Châtelet prison, accused of a new theft. This accusation was false, and he was about to be released when the Faculty of Theology demanded his retention in custody on the score of the six-year-old robbery from the College of Navarre. He came to a composition with the Faculty, whereby he was to pay them forty gold crowns a year for three years (presumably Maître Guillaume de Villon was his guarantor), and he was released.

A few weeks later Villon became involved in a street brawl, and was again arrested. He had apparently been little more than an innocent bystander; nevertheless, because of his criminal record, the authorities of the Châtelet prison took this opportunity of having him sentenced to be hanged. He appealed to Parliament, which, in a decree dated January 3rd, 1463, quashed the sentence but banished him from Paris for ten years. This is the last historical fact known of him.

ADVICE TO READERS

CLEMENT MAROT, who produced an edition of Villon's poems that was first published in 1533, less than a century after they were written, commented: 'As for the poetical worth of the bequests that Villon makes in his Testaments, in order sufficiently to perceive and understand this it would be necessary to have lived at Paris in his time, and to have known the places, things and people whereof he speaks.'

In more recent times French scholars, by means of much brilliant research into contemporary archives, have succeeded in explaining many of Villon's jokes and allusions. Nevertheless Marot's words still hold good. Jokes that need explanation, or with whose background the readers or hearers are not personally familiar, often fail to come off; and many of Villon's jokes (like many of Shakespeare's and Aristophanes') that must have provoked uproarious laughter in their time, can do so no longer.

Most of these jokes are contained in *The Bequests*, from stanza XI onwards, and in various sections of the latter half of *The Testament*. Readers who come to Villon's work for the first time are therefore advised to postpone reading these parts of it until they have read those that are poetry of lasting and universal appeal; after which they will enjoy reading the more ephemeral and parochial parts for the light they throw on Villon's character and circumstances.

J. N. C.

POEMS OF FRANÇOIS VILLON

BALLADE OF GOOD COUNSEL [1]

⟨ornament⟩

MEN of no counsel, destitute of reason,
Natures deprav'd and banish'd from good sense,
Bereft of wit, o'erflowing with unreason,
Deluded fools cramm'd with desipience,
Contriving 'gainst your own inheritance,
Who in sheer wickedness yourselves enthral
To such a death as might your hearts appal,
Doth not your shame make you repent, alas?
See what a doom doth many a lad befall
For coveting his neighbour's ox and ass.

Let each within himself see his misprision;
Seek not revenge, take all in patience:
We do perceive, this world is but a prison.
Virtuous men, free of impatience,
Know well that naught avails all violence,
To smite and wound, to pillage, kill and maul.
He fears not God, but unto Hell must crawl,
Who spends his youth in sin and evil case,
Till he at last in bitter anguish bawl
For coveting his neighbour's ox and ass.

What profits it to chouse, to laugh with treason,
To beg, to lie, to speak but in pretence,
To trick, to cog, to flatter and to poison,
To live in sin, to sleep with body tense,
To have no trust in men or confidence?

Let us, then, seek our souls in grace t' install;
Take heart anew, God be our fortress tall.
Sev'n days a week our lives are frail as glass,
And 'tis our kinsfolk have the grief and gall,
For coveting our neighbour's ox and ass.

Live we in peace and cease to bait and brawl;
Young men and old, be we united all:
The law so bids us, and th' Apostle Paul
Unto the Romans this command did pass.
Order's the staff to prop us lest we fall.
Forsake we not our true, strong city wall[2]
For coveting our neighbour's ox and ass.

THE BEQUESTS
or
THE LITTLE TESTAMENT[1]

꩜

I   IN the year fourteen fifty-six,
      I, Francis Villon, *clericus*,
      Serenely now my purpose fix,
      To celebrate that ancient use
      Recorded by Vegetius[2]
      (Sage Roman, mighty counseller),
      Profession *coram omnibus*,
      Sans which a man is wont to err.

II   It was upon th' aforesaid date,
      Near the dead season of Noël,
      When wolves have only wind for meat,[3]
      And men close by the fireside dwell,
      Out of the frost's benumbing spell,
      I had a sudden wish to break
      The very am'rous prison-cell
      Wherein my heart so long did ache.

III   And I accomplish'd my intent
      By seeing Her,[4] before my eyes,
      Giving my ruin her consent,[5]
      What though it brought her little prize:
      Wherefore I mourn, and beg the skies
      And all the gods of venery
      For vengeance on her for my sighs
      And easement of my agony.

IV   And if I thought they boded well,
Her sugar'd looks and fairest shows,
Which, though they were as false as Hell,
Could pierce my entrails – as for those,
They pay no scot for all my woes[6]
And fail me in my direst need.
On other breasts I'll seek repose,
In other gardens plant my seed.

V   Her glance hath ta'en me prisoner,
She who hath so ill-served me,
What though I did no wrong to her;
She seeks and bids that I should dree
The pangs of death, and no more be.
I see no help but to begone.
She tears her branch from my live tree,
And doth not hear my piteous moan!

VI   To spare myself a mortal wound,
'Tis best, I reckon, to depart.
Farewell! For Angers[7] I am bound,
Since unto me she'll not impart
Her favour, no, nor any part.
Through her I die, with body whole;
And thus I canonize my heart,
A martyr on the saintly roll!

VII   Sore though the parting give me grief,
I nothing can, I must begone;
As my poor wits compel belief,
Another shelters 'neath her gown;
And ne'er a herring of Boulogne
Was parch'd with saltier spleen than I.
A piteous task I'm set upon:
May God be pleas'd to hear my cry!

VIII Then, since departure is my lot,
And of return I naught can say
(I am no hero free from blot,
Nor made of steel, but common clay:
Our lives are stakes we set in play,
And death is the last coaching-stage;
The land I seek is far away),
I set these few bequests to page.

IX First, to the glory of the Father,
The Son and of the Holy Ghost,
And also of the Virgin Mother,
By whose dear grace no soul is lost,
I leave to my beloved host,
To Master Guglielmus Villon,
My name, that in his name lives most,
Also my tents and my pavilion.[8]

X Item, to Her of whom I spake,
Who thrust me from her, so unkind
That I no more delight can take
And am from ev'ry pleasure twin'd,
I leave my heart, in casket shrin'd,
Pale, piteous, defunct and chill.
My downfall was by her design'd:
God's mercy on her for that ill!

XI Item, to Ythier Marchant,[9] who
Hath put me deeply in his debt,
Or else to Master John Cornu,[9]
I leave my sword, of sharpest whet.
(It lingers in a tavern yet
As pledge for half a groat, no more.
I hereby give them leave to set
It free, when they have paid the score.)

XII   Item, to Master Saint-Amant[10]
I leave 'The White Horse' and 'The Mule'.[10]
Blaru[11] shall have mine adamant[12]
And 'The Strip'd Ass', his coach to pull.[13]
And that Decree, set out in full,
Omnis utriusque sexus,[14]
Despite the Carmelitish Bull,[14]
I leave to priests, to set in use.

XIII   Item, to Master Robert Vale,
Parliament clerk, poor needy wight[15]
(His wits, in sooth, do scarce avail),
I first of all bequeath the right
To ransom and redeem at sight
My drawers, now held at 'The Pot-Hooks',
So that his doxy Joan, bedight
In these, may truly wear the breeks.[16]

XIV   Since these alone are scarce a fit
Bequest to such a mighty man,
(The Holy Spirit lend him wit,
For, marry, there's none else who can),
I furthermore hit on the plan
To leave him 'Th' Art of Memory',[17]
(Tom Fool is now its guardian),
To stuff his brain's vacuity.

XV   Item, to yield a livelihood
To the aforesaid Master Vale
(Envy him not, in name of God!),
My heirs must sell my coat of mail,
And use the proceeds of the sale
To purchase, by the end of March,
To keep this infant plump and hale,
A scriv'ner's booth by James's church.[18]

XVI   Item, my silken cape and gloves
I give and freely do assign
To Cardon,[19] best of all my loves;
Likewise the acorn of a pine,[20]
And bid that he shall daily dine
On a fat goose, a capon tender,
Ten measures of pure, chalk-white wine
And two law-suits, to keep his slender.

XVII   Item, unto that man of rank,
René de Montigny,[21] three hounds.[22]
To John Raguier,[23] a hundred franc,
As a first charge on all my funds.
But, hold! By no means this compounds
Sums that I later may possess!
Kindness to friends must have its bounds,
Lest it should cause my heirs distress.

XVIII   Item, unto the Lord of Grigny[24]
I do bequeath the guard of Nigeon[25]
And six hounds more than to Montigny,
Likewise Bicêtre,[25] its keep and dungeon;
While as for Mouton,[26] that curmudgeon,
His rival in the witness-box,
Let him have stripes to cure his dudgeon,
And quiet lodging, in the stocks.

XIX   Item, to Master James Raguier[27]
The Popin Trough in which to soak,
The choicest cuts for his good cheer,
Young fowl and perch fresh from the brook;
Likewise 'The Pine-Cone's' inglenook:
Here let him loll, feet to the blaze,
Snug as a friar in his cloak,
With leave to wench whene'er he please.

XX   Item, to Master John Mautaint[28]
And Master Peter Basennier[28]
The grace of him[29] who doth attaint
Brawlers and rogues, and doth not spare;
To my attorney, good Fournier,[30]
Small hats and boots of supple leather,
By my own cobbler made, to cheer
And keep him warm in this cold weather.

XXI   Item, to butcher John Trouvé[31]
I leave 'The Lamb', and eke a flail
With which to chase the flies away
From 'The Wreath'd Ox', that's now on sale
Or from 'The Cow'. (Whoso should steal
This gentle beast, I dearly hope
The rogue be quickly seiz'd, and feel
Around his neck a sturdy rope!)

XXII   Next, to the Captain of the Guard
'The Helmet' henceforth appertains.[32]
His soldiers, who keep watch and ward,
Groping along those murky lanes,
Shall have two rubies for their pains –
'The Lantern', by the Milking-Stone.
But mark! if I am thrown in chains,
I'll have 'The Lilies'[33] for mine own!

XXIII   Item, I leave unto that sergeant
Known as the Bastard of the Barre,
Or sometimes as Perrenet Marchant[34] –
A merchant of the lupanar –
Three pallets, which he may prepare
To serve him at the amr'ous trade
Whereby he earns his bread, I swear,
Being for nothing better made.

XXIV Item, to Cholet and to John
   The Wolf,[35] between the two, a duck
   Captur'd, as dusk is coming down,
   Beside a ditch, by leave of luck;
   Therewith a long Franciscan cloak
   To hide the booty; wood and coals;
   Bacon and peas to spatch the cock;
   And my old gaiters lacking soles.

XXV And now, in sheer compassion,
   To three small children in distress,
   Whose names I shall set forth anon –
   Poor orphans lone and penniless,
   Barefooted and in nakedness –
   I by these presents do provide
   That they be given food and dress,
   At least throughout this wintertide.

XXVI On each – on Gerard Gossouyn,[36]
   Colin Laurens[37] and John Marceau,[38]
   Bereft of property and kin –
   I of my wealth a share bestow;
   Or else, if they prefer it so,
   Four farthings. Aye, when I am old,
   They shall not lack for food, I trow –
   Worms will supply their banquet cold![39]

XXVII Item, my nomination
   By Paris University
   I leave by resignation
   To rescue from adversity
   Poor clerks of this vicinity,
   Whose names I'll presently declare,
   Thereunto mov'd by charity
   And Nature, seeing them go bare.

XXVIII   Their names are Master William Cotin
And Master Tybalt Victry – two
Poor learned clerks who know their Latin,
Abstain from brawls and much ado; [40]
Fine singers at the lectern, too. [41]
I leave them William Gueuldry's stall, [4]
Which he shall hold from them in feu
Until on better times they fall.

XXIX   Item, they'll have a Bishop's Crook
(I mean the one in Anton's lane), [43]
Or, if they choose, a billiard-crook,
And daily a full pot of Seine.
To those poor pigeons who are ta'en
And in a sorry cage confin'd,
I leave my mirror free from stain;
And may the gaoler's wife be kind!

XXX   Item, I leave to charity
My windows hung with spiders' lace.
To every fool in pillory
I leave a buffet in the face,
And may he shiver in his place,
Lean, tousled, utterly undone,
Bare-legg'd, in tatters and disgrace,
Cold, wet and aching to the bone.

XXXI   Item, to him who cuts my hair
I leave the clippings as they lie;
To him who keeps me shod, a pair
Of rotten shoes. The frippery
May have my other finery
(When I am laid the sod beneath)
For less than what it cost to buy:
Thus charitably I bequeath.

XXXII   Item, I leave to Begging Friars,
God's Daughters and devout Béguines,
Morsels to tickle their desires,
Cakes, capons and rich galantines;
And leave to preach the Fifteen Signs[44]
And on their recompense grow fat.
(These Carmelites make concubines
Of our goodwives – but what of that?)

XXXIII   Item, I leave 'The Mortar d'Or'[45]
To John, the grocer, de la Garde,
Likewise a crutch vowed to St. Mor,
To pound his spice when it is hard.[46]
The rogue who stripp'd me of my guard,
That day when I was sorely press'd,[47]
St. Anton's fire[48] consume his lard!
To him this is my sole bequest.

XXXIV   Item, I leave to Merebeuf,[49]
And Nicholas Louviers[49] as well,
Of francs and ancient crowns enough
To cram an egge's hollow shell;
While as for Peter Rousseville,
Warden of Gouvieux,[50] such crowns
I leave to him as overspill
The pockets of the Prince of Clowns.[51]

XXXV   Finally, as I sat here writing,
At nine o'clock this night, alone
And merry, these bequests inditing,
I heard the bell of the Sorbonne,
As always at this hour, intone
The Angel's message of salvation;
Whereat I laid my labours down
To pray at my own heart's dictation.

XXXVI Then fell I in a sort of swound,
But not with wine. I know not why,
My spirit seem'd in fetters bound,
And I beheld Dame Memory
Replacing in her library
Her images collateral,
The *opinative* of truth or lie,
And others intellectual. [52]

XXXVII And furthermore th' *estimative*,
Which gives *prospective* to us all;
Similative and *formative*
(By which it often can befall
That, plagu'd by these, a man will fall,
At seasons, prey to lunacy:
This I have read, as I recall,
In Aristotle frequently).

XXXVIII Thereat the *sensitive* awoke
And thus gave *Fantasy* her head,
Who all my organs did provoke,
And yet my sovran wit in lead
Encas'd, as 'twere, beneath a dead
Pressure of sheer oblivion,
Which then throughout my being spread
To prove that all our sense is one.

XXXIX Now, with my senses back at rest,
And wits again compos'd, I think
To put an end to this bequest;
But ice hath gather'd on my ink,
My candle-flame hath ceas'd to blink,
My fire's no longer worth the tending.
Well muffled, into sleep I sink,
And can achieve no better ending.

XL Done at the time of the said date
By well-renowned Francis Villon,
Who eateth neither fig nor date.
Wrinkled and swarthy as a scullion,
He hath no tent nor no pavilion
But hath been given to some friend.
A few poor pence are all his bullion,
And these will soon be at an end.

BALLADE

(Ballade of the Blois Contest[1]*)*

～ｗ～

I D I E of thirst although the fountain's near,
As hot as fire, with icy tremors rent;
In my own land I am a foreigner;
Beside a hearth I shiver and ferment;
Bare as a worm, clad like a president,
I laugh when weeping, hope when desperate;
I have most comfort when most desolate;
I go rejoicing and am woe-begone;
I am both potent and emasculate,
Welcom'd by all, rebuff'd by everyone.

All is obscure to me save what is clear;
All is most certain save what's evident;
I have no doubt save in what doth appear;
Wisdom I hold for sudden accident;
All things I gain, and have no increment;
At break of dawn I say: 'The hour is late!'
I fear to fall, what time I lie prostrate;
I have full plenty, yet I am undone;
I'm no man's heir, yet heritance await,
Welcom'd by all, rebuff'd by everyone.

For naught I care, yet struggle to acquire
Possessions, yet am never provident.
He speaks me best who most doth flout and fleer;
He is most true who is most fraudulent;
He is my friend who maketh me consent

That swans are crows, an apple is a date;
I think men love me most when most they hate;
Lies, verities to me they are as one;
All I perceive, yet naught discriminate,
Welcom'd by all, rebuff'd by everyone.

Prince, hear the woeful tale that I relate:
Much have I learn'd, and empty is my pate;
I fear the law, yet make rebellion.
What's more to say? Restore my former state![2]
Welcom'd by all, rebuff'd by everyone.

PETITION TO MY LORD OF BOURBON[1]

 ~⚬~

M I N E own liege lord[2] and most revered prince,
 Flow'r of the Lily, of right royal blood,
Your servant Francis Villon, who doth wince
Beneath the blows of Fortune, oft renew'd,
Hereby beseeches that you think it good
To favour him with some small, gracious loan,
An obligation he will ne'er disown;
Doubt not that you shall have it back entire:
With neither loss nor interest thereon,
'Twill cost you but the time of waiting, Sire.[3]

No other prince nor lord nor Eminence
Hath he in life for such a favour woo'd.
Those half a dozen crowns you lent, long since
He hath expended solely for his food.
Both debts he'll pay at once, be't understood;
Nay, more, he'll pay them easily and soon.
If acorns yet around Patay are grown,
And if men still set chestnuts on the fire, ·
You shall have certain restitutiòn:
'Twill cost you but the time of waiting, Sire.

If I could sell my health for a few pence
To any of the Lombard brotherhood,
I do believe I'ld seize upon the chance,
So much doth lack of money vex my mood.
Cash have I none, in purse or tunic stow'd.

'Fore God! I never see a cross⁵ nor crown,
Unless it be a cross of wood or stone.
I vow and promise, let me but acquire
Such crosses as my heart is set upon,
'Twill cost you but the time of waiting, Sire.

Prince, fam'd for leaving no good deed undone,
Think you how sore it makes your servant moan
When all his hopes are trampled in the mire?
Hear me, and, if it please you, grant this boon:
'Twill cost you but the time of waiting, Sire.

THE DEBATE BETWEEN VILLON'S
HEART AND HIS BODY[1]

'What do I hear?'
                    'Tis I.'
                              'Tis who?'
                                        'Thy heart,
Who hang here only on a little thread:
And all my strength, substance and sap depart,
To see thee thus, lonely and banished,
Like a poor, beaten dog shrinking in dread.'
'Whence cometh this?'
                              'From thy own mad delight.'
'What irks it thee?'
                              ''Tis I who have the spite.'
'Nay, leave me!'
                    'Why?'
                              'I'll give thy words good thought.'
'When will that be?'
                              'When I am grown full height.'
'I'll say no more.'
                    'And I can do without.'

'What is thy wish?'
                              'To play a man's full part.'
'Hast thirty years.'
                              'Mules live so long, 'tis said.'
''Tis childhood?'
                    'Nay.'

36

'Then is it Cupid's dart
Hath pierc'd thee?'
                    'Where?'
                            'Methinks, right through the head!
Thou seest naught.'
                'Aye.'
                    'What?'
                            'A fly on bread:
'Tis plain enough: one's black, the other's white.'

And nothing more?'
                        'What more should I recite?'
'Wilt thou not yield, we'll box another bout.
Thou art undone!'
                    'Nay, first I'll show a fight.'
'I'll say no more.'
                    'And I can do without.'

'I have the sorrow: thou, the pain and smart.
Wert thou an idiot, with wits mislaid,
Thou wouldst have some excuse for this mad art;
But thou by wilful blindness hast been led.
Either thou hast a cobble-stone for head,
Or else thou takest pleasure in thy plight!
What wilt thou say, when men thee thus indict?'
'When I am dead, 'twill all be ravelled out.'
'Sage comfort! Art a very Stagirite!
I'll say no more.'
                    'And I can do without.'

'Whence comes this evil?'
                            'From the planets' chart.
When Saturn[2] on my back this burden laid,
'Twas then, methinks, my evils all did start.'

37

'*But thou art Saturn's master. Wouldst, instead,*
Become his servant? Hast thou never read
The words of Solomon:[3] *"The sage hath might*
Over the planets' benison or blight"?'
"Tis all untrue: I'll be as I was wrought.'
'*What sayst thou?*'
                          'Naught.'
                                    '*Aye, there thou speak'st aright!*
I'll say no more.'
                    'And I can do without.'

'*Dost seek to live?*'
                      'If God but grant me might!'
'*Then must thou . . .*'
                        'What?'
                                '*. . . let pangs of conscience bite.*
Study . . .'
              'In what?'
                        '*. . . in all that's true and right.*
Flee from all fools.'
                        'I'll do it, have no doubt.'
'*Remember!*'
              'Aye, thy wisdom I'll requite.'
'*Delay not, lest repentance turn to spite.*
I'll say no more.'
                    'And I can do without.'

EPISTLE[1]

❧

HAVE pity, aye, have pity upon me,
　　All ye, at least, whose friendship I did prize!
I lie beneath no may nor holly tree,
But in a dungeon under foreign skies,
One whom both God and Fortune do chastise.
Young folk and lovers, boys and damoisels,
Dancers and tumblers leaping high in reels,
Lively as darts and sharper than a thorn,
With voices ringing clear as cascabels,
Poor Villon, will you leave him there forlorn?

Ye singers carolling in lawless glee,
Ye gallants gay in word and in emprise,
Whose purses are of filthy lucre free,
Good fellows who are wittier than wise,
Ye tarry late, for all the while he dies.
Makers of music, lays and doggerels,
When he is dead, how will he need your vails?
He never sees the ev'ning or the morn:
Thick ramparts blot his vision out like scales.
Poor Villon, will you leave him there forlorn?

Behold his piteous plight, come all and see,
Noblemen free of impost and excise,
Who from no king nor emperor hold fee,
But only from the King of Paradise.
Stale bread he eats, with hunger for a spice,

So that his teeth are long as eight-inch nails,
And afterwards gulps water down from pails.
No table, nay, nor trestle doth adorn
The subterranean chamber where he swells.
Poor Villon, will you leave him there forlorn?

Princes renown'd, in suppliance he kneels:
Win pardon for him and the royal seals.
Into the light of day let him be borne.
Swine aid each other so; for, when one squeals,
The others in a herd take to their heels.
Poor Villon, will you leave him there forlorn?

BALLADE FOR FRANCE[1]

〰

MAY he encounter dragons belching fire,
  Which Jason saw, seeking the Golden Fleece,
Or change into a beast for seven year,
Like that Chaldaean king who fed on grass;
Or may he suffer such defeat and bane
As punish'd Troy for ravishing Elaine;
Or may he be engulf'd with Tantalus
And Proserpine in the infernal sloughs;
Or may he Job out-vie in sufferance,
Held captive in the tower of Daedalus,
Who wishes ill unto the realm of France!

May he be plung'd all winter in a weir,
Head foremost, like a bittern in good voice;[2]
Or ta'en and sold to the Grand Turk in hire,
Or set in harness like an ox or ass;
Or may he, like poor Mary Magdalen,
For thirty years go bare in sun and rain;
Drown like the Grecian stripling amorous;
Or hang like him whose tresses were a noose;
Or die, like Judas, of Desesperance;
Or meet the fate of Simon Magicus,
Who wishes ill unto the realm of France!

Or may he like Octavian expire,
His belly cramm'd with molten gold or brass,[2]
Or else be ground, with flesh and bones entire,
Between two millstones, as Saint Victor was;
Or may he founder choking in the main,
Like Jonah swallow'd by the great baleen.
May he be banished to Erebus
From Juno's wealth and Venus' joys profuse;
May the god Mars transfix him with his lance,
Or may he burn like Sardanapalus,
Who wishes ill unto the realm of France!

Prince, be he borne by slaves of Aeolus
To Glaucus' kingdom in the deep-sea ooze;
Or may he lose all peace and esperance:
For of such boons he is not meritous
Who wishes ill unto the realm of France.

THE TESTAMENT
or
THE GREAT TESTAMENT

❧

I   IN this my thirtieth year of age[1]
I've drunk the dregs of my disgrace,
Not all a fool, nor all a sage,
Sharp lessons though I've had to face,
Each of which sev'rally I trace
Back unto Tybalt d'Auxigny:[2]
A bishop, he, in pride and place –
That he be mine, I do deny!

II   No lord of mine nor bishop, he;
If land I hold of him, 'tis waste;
I owe him neither faith nor fee;
I'm not his vassal nor his beast.
Water and crusts were all my feast
A summer long: captive or free,
From his oppression ne'er released:
God be to him as he to me!

III   And here, if any should upbraid
And say, I utter calumnies,
Not so! If well the thing is weigh'd,
'Tis seen I slander him no wise.
Here's all the burden of my cries:
If he to me was merciful,
Sweet Jesus, King of Paradise,
Be so to him, body and soul!

43

IV   And if on me he harshly trod,
Far more than I do here recount,
I pray that the Eternal God
May serve him likewise on this count!
The Church here calls us to account,
And bids us all for foes to pray.
I'll eat my words: the full amount
Of what he did, let God assay!

V   Yes, I'll pray for him, by the shroud
Of good old Cotart![3] But, beware!
For utterance of prayers aloud
I have but little breath to spare.
I'll say for him a Picard's prayer;[4]
And, if he doth remember ill
What that may be, let him repair
To Douai, or to Flemish Lille!

VI   Yet if he truly seek to know
What prayer I'll say, then, by my Creed!
Since 'tis a favour he is slow
To ask, I shall supply his need.
I'll take my Psalter, which, indeed,
Is not bedeck'd with gold or gem,
And there the seventh verse I'll read
Out of the Psalm, *Deus laudem*.[5]

VII   Thus do I pray to God's dear Son,
To whom I cry in all my dole;
And may my piteous orison
Reach Him who gave me flesh and soul;
Who in His grace hath kept me whole
From many a hurt and vile mischance.
Him and Our Lady we extol,
And Louis, the good King of France!

VIII   To whom God grant all blessing, such
As Jacob had, or Solomon.
(Of prowess he hath all too much;
Of puissance, too, as he hath shown!)
I pray that while men dwell upon
This earth, his fame shall stay with them,
Our gracious king and paragon:
May he outlive Methusalem!⁶

IX   May twelve fine children bless his reign,
Sons of his blood majestical,
As doughty as King Charlemagne,
Conceiv'd in belly nuptial,
Courageous as Saint Martial!
Let it be with him in this wise,
Our Prince, whom may no harm befall,
And may he rest in Paradise!

X   Since lately I am sore declin'd
(Though more my means than health are spent),
Whilst I am in my perfect mind
(Or so much mind as God hath lent:
None other gives it nourishment),
I set on record, once for all,
My final Will and Testament,
Enduring and beyond recall.

XI   'Twas writ in the year sixty-one,
When I was set at liberty
From the distressful gaol of Meun
By our good monarch's clemency;
Wherefore, until the day I die,
It shall be my most happy lot
To kneel to him in vassalry;
Good deeds must never be forgot.

XII   I do confess that, after years
Of anguish'd moanings and laments,
Sorrows and agonies and fears,
Labours and grievous banishments,
I learned from all these chastisements
More than from studying by rote
That which Averroes comments
On that which Aristotle wrote.

XIII   When I was deepest in despair,
Penniless, wandering alone,
God, who did hear the pilgrims' prayer,
As in the Gospel 'tis set down,
Showed unto me a goodly town[7]
And gave the boon of Esperance:[7]
Poor sinners He doth not disown,
But hateth only obstinance.

XIV   Sinner I am, I do assent,
Yet God desireth not my death,
But only that I should repent,
And all whom sin hath in its teeth.
What though I die in sin and scathe,
God liveth and is merciful.
If I repent with my last breath,
He granteth pardon to my soul!

XV   And when *The Story of the Rose*[8]
Proclaimeth, in its op'ning part,
That pardon should be shown to those
Who in their youth are young at heart,
Since age will soon enough impart
Its lesson — why, alas! 'tis true.
But those who childe me fain would thwart
And cut my youth off ere it grew.

XVI   Were it but so, that my demise
Could something of the burden lift
That weighs on human destinies,
I swear I'd give myself short shrift!
I've done no harm, brought no ill gift
To young or old, on earth or bier:
A poor man's death will never shift
A mountain, not to fore nor rear.

XVII   When the great Alexander reign'd,
A certain man call'd Diomede
Was brought before his court, arraign'd
Of many a felonious deed,
And bound in chains, from foot to head.
He had been skill'd in piracy,
Therefore was hal'd his cause to plead,
And then to be condemn'd to die.

XVIII   The Emperor addressed him: 'Why
Art thou a robber on the main?'
To this the pirate made reply:
'Why dost thou so my trade disdain?
Because 'tis known I scour the brine
In a small, narrow ship of war?
Had I an armament like thine,
I'ld be, like thee, an emperor.

XIX   'But why lament? It is my fate
That doth so scurvily reduce
Me unto this unhappy strait.
Naught comes of struggle or abuse.
Pray furnish me with some excuse,
And think you that great poverty
(The saying is in common use)
Doth not beget great fealty.'

xx   With wonder heard the Emperor
These doughty words: 'I'll change thy fate
From bad to good,' the monarch swore,
And rais'd him to a high estate,
In which the former reprobate
Liv'd on renown'd and virtuous.
(Valerius doth the tale relate,
At Rome surnamed Maximus.)[9]

xxi   If God had given me to meet
Some other gracious Alexander
Who thus had rais'd me to my feet,
And did He then behold me wander
Back into sin, I'ld straight surrender
Myself for burning, on my soul!
Necessity drives men to plunder
And hunger sets the wolf a-prowl.

xxii   I mourn the season of my youth
(In which I revell'd more than most
Before old age had brought me ruth).
Youth drank with me no final toast;
It did not march on foot, nor post
Away on horse: how did it go?
Suddenly in the sky 'twas lost,
And left no parting gift below.

xxiii   Away it flew, and here am I,
Of wit and knowledge indigent,
Scorch'd blacker than a mulberry,
Possessing neither land nor rent.
My meanest kinsman is intent
On sundering the ties of blood
And flouting pious sentiment,
Lest I should call on him for food.[10]

XXIV Yet never have I squander'd gold
   On glutton's pleasures or debauch.
   If aught for love I ever sold,
   'Twas nothing worth my friends' reproach,
   Or naught, at most, that overmuch
   Could burden them or cause distress.
   Such calumnies I hereby scotch:
   A blameless man need naught confess.

XXV True, I have lov'd, and think no shame,
   And willingly would love again;
   But grieving heart and empty wame,
   Which never can its fill obtain,
   Have banish'd me from love's domain.
   Let him who well hath drunk and din'd
   Endure love's arduous campaign:
   He danceth best whose belly's lin'd.

XXVI Ah, God! Had I, in my mad youth,
   Been subject unto virtue's rule
   And studied hard, by now, in sooth,
   I'd have my house and sleep on wool.
   But, fie upon 't! I fled from school
   Like any other erring son . . .
   As I set down these words, poor fool,
   My heart nigh breaks to think thereon.

XXVII Too well I heard the soft advice
   (It brought me to a pretty pass)
   The Preacher giveth: 'Son, rejoice
   That thou art young.' But out, alas!
   Elsewhere he sings another mass,
   When he in solemn words declares
   That *vanitatum vanitas*,
   Youth and its pleasures are but snares.

XXVIII 'My days,' saith Job, 'are gone for ever,
Utterly taken from the land,
Like threads of cloth to which the weaver
Swiftly applies a burning brand.'
Each straying morsel by his hand
Is caught away, and vanisheth.
Therefore no more in fear I stand,
For all will be assuag'd by death.

XXIX Where are they now, those dear young folk
I knew so well in days of old,
They who so sweetly sang and spoke,
In word and deed so gay and bold?
Many today are stiff and cold,
Nothing of them is now surviving.
May they have peace in Heaven's fold,
And God have mercy on the living!

XXX And some of those who are not dead,
Are now, praise God! great lords and masters;
Others go bare and beg for bread –
Vainly, the poor, unwilling fasters;
Others are lolling in the cloisters
Celestine or Carthusian,
Booted as if they fish'd for oysters:
So varied is the lot of man!

XXXI As for the first, the high and splendid,
I'll only pray, God give them grace:
Since they have nothing to be mended,
Silence is golden in their case.
For those in want and in disgrace,
Like me, God help them to endure!
For monks all pray'r were out of place:
Their bread and pittance are secure.

XXXII   Good wines they have, full often broach'd,
Sauces and broths, fish of great size,
Tarts and cream cakes, eggs fried or poach'd,
Scrambled, or in some other guise.
The mason, as his trade he plies,
Hath journeymen at his command.
The monk, he toileth otherwise:
He poureth wine with his own hand.

XXXIII   Yet all this mockery is idle,
And freely I do make retraction.
I'm not a magistrate or beadle
Set up for other men's correction.
No wight is further from perfection
Than I, who thank the Lord for it!
Let this afford them satisfaction;
But that which I have writ, is writ.

XXXIV   Let us leave sleeping dogs at rest
And speak of matters more delighting.
Such stuff is not to ev'ry taste,
'Tis tedious and uninviting.
Poverty, venomous and biting,
Into rebellious envy sinks;
Ever it must be rudely flyting,
And what it dares not say, it thinks.

XXXV   All my life long I have been poor,
Of poor and lowly origin.
My father never had much store
Of wealth, nor any of my kin.
Poverty always crank'd us in.
The tombs 'neath which my forebears lie
Record no prince nor paladin:
May God receive their souls on high!

XXXVI   As I bemoan my wretched state,
        I often hear my heart upbraid:
        'Man, do not be so desolate,
        Nor of thy grief make such parade.
        Wert thou so utterly decay'd
        As poor James Cœur,[11] couldst be content
        Not to be some dead lord who's laid
        To rot beneath a monument.'

XXXVII A lord, and dead! What do I say?
        A lord, alas! and not so now?
        Remember we the Psalmist's lay:
        'His place no longer shall him know.'
        What follows after that, I vow,
        Is no concern of mine, a sinner.
        'Tis a grave matter, I'll allow:
        Let priests discuss it after dinner.

XXXVIII That which I am, full well I know –
        No angel's kin; upon my head
        No starry diadem doth glow.
        My father, rest his soul, is dead,
        His body 'neath the waves[12] is laid . . .
        My mother soon will die – and, marry,
        She knows it, I do greatly dread.
        The son will not much longer tarry.

XXXIX   I know that, be they rich or poor,
        Wiseman or madman, priest or lay,
        Noble or serf, burgess or boor,
        Spendthrift or miser, sad or gay,
        Ladies in great or mean array,
        Of whatsoe'er condition,
        Death taketh all of them away,
        And maketh no exception.

52

XL   Be 't Paris's or Helen's death,
Whoever dies, he dies in smart
So great, he lacketh wind and breath;
His gall breaks in upon his heart,
And from his brow the sweat doth start —
God knows what sweat! And none will aid,
For there is none would take his part
And go as hostage in his stead.

XLI   Death makes his body lean and pale;
It crooks his nose, distends each vein,
Bloats up his neck. His flesh is frail,
His joints and sinews bulge and strain.
Ah, woman's body, so urbane,
Tender and smooth and sensitive,
Must you, then, suffer all this pain?
Aye, or go heavenwards alive!

BALLADE
(*Ballade of the Ladies of bygone time*)

T E L L me but where, beneath what skies
Is lovely Roman Flora ta'en?
Tell me where Archipiada[13] lies,
Or Thais[14] (they were kin, these twain);
Or Echo, answering again
Across the river and the mere,
Beauty of more than human strain?
Where are the snows of yesteryear?[15]

Where is the learned Eloise,
For whom Pierre Abelard, her swain,
Became a monk at Saint Denis,
And had for her his manhood slain?

53

Where is the queen who did ordain
That Buridan, her sometime dear,
Should perish coldly in the Seine?
Where are the snows of yesteryear?

Queen Blanche, white as a fleur-de-lys,
Who sang like sirens o'er the main?
Bertha the Broadfoot, Beatrice,
Or Erembourg who held the Maine;
Or Joan, sweet lady of Lorraine,
For whom the English drop no tear:
Where are they, Virgin sovereign?
Where are the snows of yesteryear?

Prince,[16] do not ask where they are lain,
Ask not the week, ask not the year,
Lest you remember this refrain:
Where are the snows of yesteryear?

ANOTHER BALLADE

(*Ballade of the Lords of bygone time*[17])

NAY more, where is the third Calixt,[a]
Last of his name to sit the throne,
Who four years held the papalist?
Alfonso, King of Aragon?[b]
That well-lov'd Duke, he of Bourbon?[c]
Artus, the ruler of Britaine,[d]
The seventh Charles,[e] surnam'd 'le bon'?
Where is the doughty Charlemagne?

That King of Scots[f] of whom we wist
The tale that half his visage shone
As purple as an amethyst
From brow to chin? That paragon,
The King of Cyprus?[g] Answers none,
Alas? And that good King of Spain[h]
Whose name I shall recall anon?
Where is the doughty Charlemagne?

From further asking I'll desist;
This world is but deception.
'Gainst death no mortal can resist,
Nor find nor seek protection.
One question more, and I have done:
Bohemia's Ladislas[18] – explain,
Where's he? Where is his grandsire gone?
Where is the doughty Charlemagne?

Where is Du Guesclin[19] ridden on?
Where's the Count Dauphin of Auvergne?[20]
Where's the brave Duke of Alençon?[21]
Where is the doughty Charlemagne?

ANOTHER BALLADE
(*Couched in Old French, in the original*[22])

E'EN if it be that blessed soul,
The Pope, with alb and rosary,
(Who, when he prays, must wear a stole
In which to snare The Enemy
So hot with hate and mockery),
He dies like nobleman or hind,
Out of this world puff'd suddenly:
Such stuff is carried down the wind.

55

Gold-fisted soldans who control
Constantinople's empery;
Or he of France, whom we extol
Above all others' monarchy;
Who, in his godly piety
Churches and convents hath design'd:
If they in life had majesty,
Such stuff is carried down the wind.

Be't Dauphins of Vienne, Grenobles,
In battle bold, in council sly,
Lords of Dijon, Salins and Dôle,
The sires and eldest progeny;
Or be't their trains of chivalry –
Stout men-at-arms who've drunk and din'd,
Trumpeters, heralds, yeomanry:
Such stuff is carried down the wind.

Princes, ye too are doom'd to die,
With all the rest of humankind.
If ye are vex'd or griev'd thereby,
Such stuff is carried down the wind.

XLII   Since popes and kings and sons of kings,
Conceived in the wombs of queens,
Do turn to chill and mouldy things,
And unto others yield their reigns,
Shall I, poor peddling wight of Rennes,[23]
Not also die? Yes, if God will.
To him who first some pleasure gleans
An honest death comes as no ill.

XLIII   Not everlasting is this life,
However wealthy rogues resent it.
Over us all there hangs a knife.
Poor aged man, be thou contented:
They who, when thou wert young, assented
To all thy mocking quips, would scold
Thee now as knavish and demented
If thou shouldst mock when thou art old.

XLIV   So let him take to beggary,
Since fate thereto doth him constrain.
Day after day he longs to die;
His heart is eaten by such pain
That, but for fear of God, he fain
Would violate God's own command
And blot his soul with dreadful stain,
Taking his life by his own hand.

XLV   Though many would applaud his japes
In youth, yet now they have no place.
Men hate an aged jackanapes
And cannot brook his least grimace.
And if, to please, he hold his peace,
They scorn him as an empty fool;
And if he speak, they bid him cease
Or take his prattle back to school.

XLVI   Likewise it is with some poor trull
Left in old age and penury,
Who sees the market-places full
Of younger girls who publicly
Flaunt their fresh wares, and asks God why
She first saw light so long ago;
And God, He maketh no reply,
Nor will rebuke her in her woe.

THE TESTAMENT

(*The lament of the fair Heaulmière*[24])

METHINKS I hear the harlot wail
Who was the helmet-maker's lass,
Wishing herself still young and hale,
And crying in her woe: 'Alas!
Old Age, so cruel and so crass,
Why hast thou struck me down so soon?
What holds me back that, in this pass,
I do not seek death's final boon?

'Hast robb'd me of that mighty sway
Which beauty gave me at my birth
O'er all men, clerical or lay.
Once there was not a man on earth
But would have given all his worth,
Could he but win of me that prize
Which now, in these my days of dearth,
Even the beggars do despise.

'There's many a man I could have had,
But flouted, in my foolishness,
For love of a sharp-witted lad
On whom I shower'd my largesse.
Others might buy a feign'd caress:
'Twas he I lov'd, more than myself,
Whom he did cruelly oppress,
And lov'd me only for my pelf.

'And yet his bitterest attack
Could never cause my love to die.
He could have dragg'd me on my back
Or trampled me – did he but cry

"Kiss me!" away my woes would fly.
That beast, that slimy manikin,
Would cuddle me . . . And what have I
Left for it all? Disgrace and sin!

'Well, thirty years ago he died,
And I am left here, old and hoar.
When I bethink my days of pride,
What I am now, and was of yore,
Or when I hold a glass before
My naked body, now so chang'd,
Wrinkled and shrunken, frail and poor,
My wits with grief are nigh estrang'd.

'Where is that forehead's fair expanse;
That golden hair; those arching brows;
Those wide-set eyes; that pretty glance,
With which I charm'd the most morose;
Those little ears; that dainty nose,
Neither too tiny nor too great;
That dimpled chin; those Cupid's bows
Of lips; those teeth so white and straight?

'Where are the shoulders neat and slender;
Those long, soft arms; those fingers brent;
Those little breasts; those haunches tender,
High-rais'd and smooth and plainly meant
For riders in love's tournament;
Those ample loins, firm thighs, and twat
Set like a graceful monument
Within its handsome garden-plot?

The forehead scowls, the hair is grey,
The brows are gone, the eyes are blear
That were so mocking and so gay
They fill'd the passers-by with cheer;

THE TESTAMENT

The nose is hook'd and far from fair,
The ears are rough and pendulous,
The face is sallow, dead and drear,
The chin is purs'd, the lips hang loose.

Aye, such is human beauty's lot!
The arms are short; the hands clench tight;
The shoulders tangle in a knot;
The breasts, in shame they shrink from sight;
Nipple and haunch, they share their plight;
The twat – ah, bah! The thighs are thin
As wither'd hams, and have a blight
Of freckles, like a sausage-skin.

'Tis thus we mourn for good old days,
Perch'd on our buttocks, wretched crones,
Huddled together by the blaze
Of some poor fire of forest cones,
That dies as quickly as our moans,
A briefly-lit, brief-living flame –
We who have sat on lovers thrones! . . .
With many a man 'tis just the same.

BALLADE

(*The belle Heaulmière to all wenches*)

SWEET Glover, bear my words in mind
(My pupil, once, adroit and bold),
And you, Blanche Cobbler: soon you'll find
How well I have your fortune told.
Take payment for the wares you've sold;
No mercy upon men, say I!
You're naught to them, when you are old,
But coin the officers decry.[25]

Dear Sausager, who are so kind
And dance so well, dance as you're told!
Gillian Weaver, be resigned,
Let not your masters hear you scold.
Too soon your blinds will be unroll'd,
When you are wither'd up and dry.
Some aged priest is all you'll hold
With coin the officers decry.

Jennifer Hood, be not inclin'd
To check your gallops o'er the wold!
Catherine Purser, be not blind;
Keep your men safe within the fold.
Girls who their dalliance withhold
Provoke not wrath, but mockery.
Horrid old age doth turn men cold,
Like coin the officers decry.

Wenches, give ear while I unfold
The reason why I weep and cry:
The years have so debas'd my gold,
'Tis coin the officers decry.

XLVII   Such was the sermon she did preach,
That beauty of a bygone date
(Whatever moral it may teach.
Another writes as I dictate,
My scribe, poor Firmin Addlepate.[26]
I've been as careful as I can.
If he write false, I'll be irate:
The master's measur'd by the man.)

XLVIII   Thus I perceive the mighty danger
That doth beset an am'rous wight;
And if some disputatious stranger
Should say to me: 'Nay, think aright!
If you recoil from love, in fright
At the deceits of them you name,
You are the merest Bedlamite,
For these are women of ill fame.

XLIX   'What if they sell us love for cash?
Our love for them is no less cheap.
They kiss and fondle any trash,
And laugh when most our purses weep.
Far otherwise our comradeship
With women of high reputation!
With these a bachelor should keep,
And not with wenches of low station.'

L   He who so speaks doth not surprise,
Nor yet doth not persuade me, neither.
'Love but the chaste and good,' he cries.
(I fancy I can hear him blether.)
Aye, but we well might question whether
The little women of the stews,
With whom I pass whole days together,
Would not be chaste, if they could choose.

LI   Chaste? Aye, they all were that, in youth,
Unspotted by reproach or blame.
In the beginning, if the truth
Be fully known, each little dame
Made sacrifice of her good name,
With merchant, monk or muleteer,
Only to quench love's raging flame,
That worse than Anton's itch[27] doth sear.

LII   Nay more, their lads held the Decree[28]
In reverence, as doth appear:
They hid their love, each he and she;
Their pleasures none but they did share.
But such a love doth quickly bear
An host of loves: from the first lover
She takes her leave, and doth repair
To any loves whom chance discover.

LIII   What doth so move the female creature?
I wish to speak no calumnies,
But think it be in woman's nature
To long to share the vivid joys
Of loving with all men and boys.
They say at Reims – and they agree
At Lille and Saint-Omer and Troyes:
Six craftsmen do more work than three.

LIV   Well, silly swains are struck in volley,[29]
The ladies hie themselves away.
All ends in faithlessness and folly:
Such is a lover's final pay,
Whate'er the sweetness of a day.
'With dogs or birds, in love or fight,'
As men so oft unthinking say,
'A hundred griefs to one delight!'

(Double Ballade)

Love, therefore, as you please; go fling
Yourselves in dance or celebration.
Your frolics no reward will bring
But ruin and annihilation.
Mad love begetteth a mad nation;
King Solomon was in its thrall;
Samson was lur'd to excecation.
Happy is he who flouts them all!

Orpheus the minstrel, who could sing
And play to all men's delectation,
Almost became an offering
To Cerberus, by love's oblation.
Narcissus, through infatuation,
Into a well did swooning fall,
Enamour'd of enamoration.
Happy is he who flouts them all!

The doughty knight Sardana, king
Of all the Cretan population,
Sought to become a neuter thing
And join with lasses at filation.
David, though skill'd in divination,
Saw two fair thighs, and straight did crawl
In sin, forgetting his salvation.
Happy is he who flouts them all!

Ammon, by feigned hankering
For tarts, achiev'd the defloration
Of his own sister, and did bring
Her to incestuous relation.

Herod – 'tis no exaggeration –
Was coax'd by dancer's wiles to call
For Baptist John's decapitation.
Happy is he who flouts them all!

*

Let my own fate be epilogue,[30]
Who, as I shall not shrink to tell,
Was stripp'd and beaten like a rug.
Who set this trap in which I fell?
Who else but Catherine Vausselles?[31]
'Twas a fine wedding festival;[32]
The bridegroom's friend was false Noël.[33]
Happy is he who flouts them all!

But would you have yon gallant spurn
Yon dames, and give them all wide room?
Not if he were condemn'd to burn
Like one who rides upon a broom!
Sweeter than honey in the comb
Are they to him; but should he fall
To trusting them, he earns his doom.
Happy is he who flouts them all!

LV If she who held me in her fief,
In vassalage obedient,
And caus'd me so much pain and grief
And did most cruelly torment,
Had but reveal'd the true intent
That lay behind her sugar'd looks,[34]
Why then, indeed, I would have spent
Some pains to save me from her hooks.

LVI Whatever I might choose to say,
She was full well inclin'd to hear,
And gave me neither yea nor nay.
More, she would suffer me come near
And press myself against her chair,
And thus her lover did beguile
All his true passion to declare;[34]
But, ah! 'twas nothing but a wile!

LVII She did my wits so sorely hash
That she could make me think, whenever
She chose to cheat, that flour was ash,
A velvet bonnet was a beaver,
Old iron dross was purest silver,
An ambesace a double three.
(Thus always an adroit deceiver
Can make men doubt the things they see.)

LVIII The sky could be a copper gong;
A heap of clouds a calveskin;
The morning could be evensong;
A cabbage-stalk could be a vine,
Flat, filthy ale the purest wine;
A sow could be a watermill,
A hangman's noose a silken skein,
A fat old priest a brandish'd bill!

LIX Thus love deceiv'd me, love that can
Make night of day and day of night.
I do believe that any man,
E'en though his wits were silver-bright,
Would lose his raiment in this fight,
And be thereafter thrust aside,
Like me, who ev'rywhere am hight
'The lover cast-off and denied'.

LX And Love, in turn, I do disown;
  To war and flame I challenge it!
  Death, in Love's person, hurls me down,
  And neither of them cares a whit.
  Old Adam, hence! I shall submit
  No longer to the name of lover;
  For if the title did befit
  Me once, I swear those days are over.

LXI Let those pursue the fight who deem
  It worth the anguish; not so I!
  I'll say no more upon this theme,
  But keep my promise faithfully.
  If any seek the reason why,
  Or marvel at the man who dares
  To rail at Love, I make reply:
  A man should well instruct his heirs.

LXII My throat is parch'd with bitter gall,
  I spit as white as eiderdown,
  Gobs bigger than a tennis-ball.
  What means all this? That Kate and Joan
  Think me no more a gay young loon,
  But an old, broken-winded jade.
  I have an old man's voice and tone,
  Though still, at heart, a ruffling blade.

LXIII God and Tack Tybalt[35] most I thank,
  Who mur'd me in a dungeon low,
  Where I so much cold water drank
  And fed upon the pear of woe,[36]
  Enchain'd – when I remember how,
  I pray for him, *et reliqua*,[37]
  That God may grant him . . . aye, just so,
  I quite agree . . . *et cetera.*

LXIV   Yet, all despite, I bear no hate
For him, nor his lieutenant, neither,
Nor yet for his judge-advocate,
Who is as pleasant[38] as fair weather.
The rest have slipp'd my mem'ry's tether,
Saving the executioner,
Young Bob:[39] I love them all together,
As God doth love an usurer!

LXV   As I recall, five years ago
Certain bequests, when first I went
Forth from this town, I did bestow,
Which some, who had not my consent,
Were pleas'd to style a 'Testament':
The name's not mine, but theirs alone.
'Tis all too plainly evident,
No man is master of his own.

LXVI   These gifts I seek not to withhold,
E'en though the cost of them should mar
My whole estate. I'm not yet cold
Towards the Bastard of the Barre.[40]
Besides my pallets, I declare
That he shall have my aged mats,
To hold him perpendicular
When on his two hind legs he squats.

LXVII   If there be any who can show
He hath not had his full bequest,
To Turgis,[41] Provins[42] and Moreau[43]
All his complaints should be address'd
(Supported by my strict behest).
These are my heirs residuary,
Who own whate'er I once possess'd,
Unto the bed on which I lie.

LXVIII   Now I shall say but one word more,
For I am eager to testate.
To Firmin,[44] who, unless he snore,
Doth hear my words, I now dictate:
No man shall suffer in estate
Through this my present ordinance,
The which must not be promulgate
Elsewhere than in the realm of France.

LXIX   I feel my heart is growing feeble,
My parlance is no longer clear.
Firmin,[45] be seated; fetch the table
Close to my bed, that none may hear;
Bring pen and ink and paper near;
Set down the substance of my meaning,
Then copy out the text in fair;
And let us start at the beginning.

LXX   Now, in God's name, Father eternal,
And of the Son, sweet Mary's flow'ret,
God with the Father coeternal,
Together with the Holy Spirit,
Through whom we shed the sin we herit
From Adam, and do Heav'n adorn . . .
He who believes, not small his merit,
That saints of corpses can be born!

LXXI   Dead are their souls and mortal frames,
And damned to perditiòn:
Their flesh is clay, their souls are flames,
Whate'er was their conditiòn.
Yet I do make exceptiòn
Of ev'ry patriarch and prophet;
For, as is my conceptiòn,
Their rumps were never warm'd in Tophet.

LXXII   Should any offer me a smart
Rebuke: 'How dar'st thou vaunt so high
Thine own surmises, thou who art
No Master of Theology?',
On Jesus' fable I rely,
Of Dives whom his sins did damn
Deep in the fires of Hell to fry,
Whilst Lazar couch'd with Abraham.

LXXIII   If Lazar's finger had been burning,
Dives would ne'er have thus besought
A drop of water from it, yearning
To slake his gullet's fearful drought.
Well may they tremble at the thought,
Bibbers who drink their shirts away,
Since wine is all too dearly bought,
God save us – I speak not in play!

LXXIV   Once more, in God's thrice holy Name,
And of His glorious Mother, too,
(Let me set nothing down in blame,
Though thin enough to scare a crow:
If I escape a sudden throe
Of rage, 'tis but by grace Divine.)
Concerning many a loss and woe
I hold my peace, and thus begin.

LXXV   First, my poor soul I do commend
Unto the blessed Trinity,
And may Our Lady be its friend,
The Chamber of Divinity.
I beg the angels' charity,
That they, in full procession
Of all their ninefold Hierarchy,
May bear this gift before the Throne.

LXXVI Item, my body I assign
　　　Unto our mighty mother earth:
　　　(The worms thereon shall scantly dine:
　　　'Twas too much warr'd upon by dearth.)
　　　Right yarely bring it to its berth:
　　　From earth it came, to earth must go.
　　　All things that know whence came they forth
　　　Do willingly return thereto.

LXXVII Item, unto my more than father,
　　　To Master Guglielmus V.
　　　(More loving-kindness than a mother
　　　Shows to her babe, show'd he to me:
　　　From many a broil he set me free,
　　　And took therein but little joy)
　　　I do beseech, upon my knee,
　　　He give himself no more annoy.

LXXVIII To him I leave my library,
　　　Which doth comprise the *Pet au Deable*,[46]
　　　A tale that Master Tabarie[47]
　　　Engross'd, a man most veritable.[48]
　　　It lies in heaps beneath a table;
　　　And though the style be poor and rough,
　　　The matter is so memorable,
　　　It offers recompense enough.

LXXIX Item, for my beloved mother
　　　A certain pray'r I have inscroll'd.
　　　She, for my sake, hath many a pother,
　　　God knows, and many an anguish thol'd.
　　　I have no citadel nor hold
　　　Where I can flee, in my distress
　　　Of soul and body manifold,
　　　But her, that aged pauperess!

BALLADE

(*A ballade in prayer to Our Lady*)

LADY of Heav'n, God's Regent over man
And Empress over the infernal mere,
Receive Thou me, Thine humble Christian,
That I may dwell with them thou holdest dear,
Though naught at all have I deserved here.
Such grace as Thine, Lady and Governess,
Doth far outweigh my human sinfulness;
That grace sans which (I know, and tell no lie)
No soul can e'er aspire to saintliness.
'Tis in this faith I mean to live and die.

Say to Thy Son, I serve him as I can,
That He may cause my sins to disappear,
As once He pardon'd the Egyptian,
Or eke that cleric whom He did not ban
From mercy, but Thy plea for him did hear,
What though the Devil held him in duress.
Preserve Thou me from such a wickedness,
Virgin who bore, in unstain'd sanctity,
The Host we duly celebrate at Mass.
'Tis in this faith I mean to live and die.

I'm but a poor old woman, small and wan;
Naught have I read, of naught am well aware.
In church the painted images I scan
Of Paradise, and also of a drear
Place where the wicked boil: these make me fear,
Those others give me joy and happiness.
Grant that the joy be mine, Thou Holiness
To Whose protection sinners all should fly;
Crown me with faith, sans feint or idleness:
'Tis in this faith I mean to live and die.

V irgin who bore, most virtuous princess,
J esus whose reign o'er men shall never cease,
L ord who assum'd our mortal feebleness,
L eft Heav'n and to succour us drew nigh,
O ffering death his young, sweet loveliness.
N ow such Our Lord is, such I him confess.
'Tis in this faith I mean to live and die.

LXXX   Item I leave my love, my rose,
No part of me, nor heart nor liver.
There's much that she'ld prefer to those
Although she hath no lack of silver.
What were a better thing to give her?
A purse, with crowns to fill its wame!
But hang the man who gives a stiver,
And hang me if I do the same!

LXXXI   For, sure, she doth not lack for bread;
But that's the least of all my cares.
My greatest griefs for her are dead,
My buttocks carry no more scars.
I leave her charge to Michaut's heirs,
Known as the Great Adulterer.
Beside his tomb go say your prayers,
At Saint Satur[49] below Sancerre.

LXXXII   But nonetheless, to pay my debt
(My debt to Love, be't understood,
And not to her, who never let
Me hope at all, howe'er I woo'd.
I know not whether she withstood
All other men; but I declare
That now, by Jesus' holy Rood,
I do but laugh at the affair.)

LXXXIII The following Ballade I send,
With rhymes that terminate in R.
Who'll carry it? Let me perpend . . .
None else than Pernet de la Barre![50]
Who, when he see her from afar,
My damsel with the crooked neb,
Must say, in the vernacular:
'Whence comest thou, thou filthy drab?'

BALLADE

(*Ballade to his mistress*)

F alse beauty who, although in semblance fair,
R ude art in action, and hast cost me dear,
A s iron harsh, and harder to outwear,
N ame that did spell the end of my career,
C harm that dost mischief, builder of my bier,
O gress who dost thy lover's death require,
Y outh without pity! Womankind, dost hear?
S hould help a man, not drag him in the mire!

M uch better had it been to seek elsewhere
A id and repose, and keep my honour clear,
R ather than thus be driven by despair
T o flee in anguish and dishonour drear.
'*H* elp, help!' I cry. 'Ye neighbours all, draw near;
E ach man fetch water for my raging fire!'
Compassion bids that every true compeer
Should help a man, not drag him in the mire.

V anished soon will be thy beauty rare,
I [51]ts blossom will be withered and sere.
I [51] could find cause for laughter, were I there,
L iving and eating still. But nay, 'twere sheer
L unacy, for by then I'ld be thy peer,
O ld, ugly as thyself, and sans desire
N ow drink amain! For drinking and good cheer
Should help a man, not drag him in the mire.

Prince of all lovers, I do scarcely dare
To ask thine aid, lest I provoke thine ire;
But ev'ry honest heart, by God I swear,
Should help a man, not drag him in the mire.

LXXXIV   Item, to Master Ythier Marchant[52]
        (To whom I left my sword, to pay
        A debt that honour held most urgent),
        I leave a ten-line roundelay.
        Let him set music to 't, and play
        A lute therewith, to celebrate
        His onetime love – I shall not say
        Her name, or I would earn his hate.

LAY

    DEATH, of thy rigour I complain:
    Hast ravished my mistress hence,
    And wilt not yet show penitence,
    But holdest me in swooning pain,
    With all my vital forces ta'en.
    How did her life give thee offence,
        Death?

We had one heart between the twain:
If she be dead, it follows thence
That I must die, or in pretence
Live on, like images that feign
        Death!

LXXXV   Item, to Master John Cornu
I wish to make a new bequest,
Because his friendship is so true
Whenever I am sore distress'd:[53]
I leave him, then, the summer nest
I have of Master Baubignon,[54]
If he will promise to make fast
The rooftree, which is falling down.

LXXXVI   I've lost a whetstone and a pick,
Because it lacks a door, that house.
Inside, the darkness is so thick,
Ten owls could scarcely catch a mouse.
'Tis open wide to any chouse.
I put a jenny[55] up for sign;
And whosoe'er stole *that*, the louse,
May he find spittle in his wine!

LXXXVII   Item, whereas the gracious wife
Of Master Peter Saint Amant[56]
(If she hath sinn'd, in all her life,
I pray that God be tolerant!)
Hath cleped me a mendicant,[56]
A new bequest shall be his share:
In place of steeds right elegant,[57]
He'll have a jackass and a mare.

LXXXVIII   Item, Sire Denis Hesselin,[58]
Burgess of Paris, I apparel
With fourteen casks of Aulnis wine
Taken from Turgis[59] at my peril.
But if he drink enough to quarrel
With his good sense and probity,
Let them put water in each barrel:
Wine ruins many a family.

LXXXIX   Item, unto mine advocate,
Master Charruau,[60] I bequeath
My sword[60] (which Marchant had of late)[61] . . .
I shall say nothing of the sheath![62]
Also a *royal d'or* therewith –
But this, to make his purse more ample,
Shall be in halfpence, strewn beneath
The trees and bushes of the Temple.

XC   Item, that worthy man of law,
Fournier, so oft my champion,
Four fistfuls from my purse may draw;
For many a cause of mine he won –
Just causes all, by God's dear Son!
And proven so, I'm glad to state:
But then, when all is said and done,
Good cause deserves good advocate.

XCI   Item, I leave to Master Jack
Raguier[63] 'The Goblet' on the Strand.
But he shall pay four farthings back
(Even though first he must have pawn'd
His gaiters) if he ever stand
Or sit to drink, and do not look
To see if I be close at hand,
In the old Pine-Cone's inglenook.[63]

XCII   Item, concerning Merebeuf
And also Nicholas de Louviers,[64]
I leave them neither cow nor beef,
For they're not fated to be drovers,
But rather to be lordly lovers
Of falconry,[65] and cry halloo
In quest of partridges and plovers
Sold by the Widow Machecoue.[66]

XCIII   Item, if Turgis[67] but present
His bill, I'll pay without a fight.
(If he can find my tenement,
He must be blessed with second-sight.)
I leave him th' aldermanic right[68]
To which, as Paris-born, I'm heir,
Though speaking with an accent slight
Of Poitiers, having learnt it there.[69]

XCIV   From two sweet ladies, kind and fair,
Residing at Saint Générou,
Hard by Saint Julien, which is near
The Breton March or in Poitou.[70]
But why should I reveal to you
Just where these ladies pass their days?
Such things a wise man doth eschew
To babble in the market-place.

XCV   Item, to John Raguier I give
(A sergeant of the Twelve,[71] forsooth!),
For ev'ry day while he's alive,
A cheesecake, succulent and smooth,
In which to plunge a greedy tooth,
Upon the cost of Master Bailly;[72]
And afterwards, to slake his drouth,
A pint of Maubuay,[73] three times daily.

XCVI   Item, unto the Prince of Clowns[74]
I leave du Four, that great buffoon,[75]
Whose quips are fam'd in many towns;
And well he sings *The lover's boon.*
I wish him a good afternoon,
For, when he's in a mood for jest,
He is a proper, lazy loon;
But 'tis his absence pleaseth best.

XCVII   Item, to the Eleven Score,[76]
Who such a fine example set
And are good friends to rich and poor
(Notably Richier and Vallette),
To each a gibbet-rope, to plait
Around his beaver. But, of course,
This gift is to the Foot; as yet
I've had no dealings with the Horse.

XCVIII   Again, I leave to Perrenet
(I mean the Bastard of the Barre,[77]
Who is my darling and my pet),
Upon his shield, in place of bar,
Three loaded dice, to help his star,
And cards well mark'd. But if he ever
Let flee a fart where men can hear,
I've one more gift: a quartan fever.

XCIX   Item, it is my wish that Cholet[78]
No longer ply the copper's trade.
Of all his tools, except his mallet,
Let general exchange be made
Against a trusty Lyons blade.
He is not one to brawl or curse
Or ruffle, but, if truth be said,
From small disputes he's not averse.

C   Item, to John the Wolf,[78] a man
Upright and just in ev'ry matter,
But, for the chase, too thin and wan
(And Cholet, too, is scarce a better
Huntsman than he), I leave a setter –
A hound that in its path of duty
Leaves not a single fowl a-flutter;
Likewise a cloak, to hide the booty.

CI   Item, I leave unto that swinger
Known as The Wooden Aurifex,[79]
A hundred spikes of Syrian ginger,[80]
Not to add merely box to box,
But to bring arses unto cocks
And puddings unto female groins,
That milk may rise 'neath women's smocks,
And blood flow down into men's loins.

CII   Item, to Captain John Riou,[81]
Both for himself and for his archers,
I leave six wolves' heads in a stew
(A meat that is not fit for poachers),
Seiz'd from those mastiffs known as butchers
And cook'd in sauce of poor man's wine.
He who would eat such filthy creatures
Would shrink from no foul deed, the swine.

CIII   It is a somewhat heavy meat,
Scarcely as light as cork or down,
Though doubtless good enough to eat
In tents or some beleaguer'd town.

If they were snar'd, not overthrown
In chase (since mastiffs have no care
For hunting[82]) let him make a gown
Of mastiffs' hides, for his own wear.[83]

CIV   Item, to Robinet Trascaille,[84]
Who fareth well in life, good lad,
And is no runner like a quail,
But rides upon a sturdy pad,
I leave a bowl on which he had
A greedy eye this many a year.
Now he needs nothing more to add
Completeness to his household gear.

CV   Next, on Girard I hereby settle
(Of Bourg-la-Reine a barber loyal)[85]
Two shaving-basins and a kettle:
He earns his bread with so much toil![85]
Six years ago with bel-accoil
He harbour'd me, and bade me dine
(Witness the Abbess of Port-Royal)[86]
A se'night long on fatten'd swine.

CVI   Item, unto the Mendicants,
God's Daughters and devout Béguines,
Wherever be their chosen haunts,
To Turlupins and Turlupines,[87]
Of cheesy soup and galantines
And rich cream tarts I make oblation;
And later, when they've drawn the screens,
Let them discourse of contemplation!

CVII   But this, in truth is no bequest
        Of mine, but comes from all men's mothers,
        Also from God, who thus hath blest
        The monks for all their pains and pothers.
        They sure must live, the goodly Fathers,
        E'en those of the Parisian houses.
        If they make sport with wives of others,
        'Tis for the love they bear their spouses.

CVIII   Whatever Master John Poullieu[88]
        Did seek to say, and more beside,
        Shamefully and in public view
        Perforce his meaning he denied.
        Master de Meung[89] did much deride
        Their ways, as did Matheolus.[90]
        But we must honour those the Bride
        Of God appointeth over us.

CIX   Therefore I bow to them as servant,
        In all that I can do or say
        Of their high rank and worth observant,
        And daring not to disobey.
        That man is mad who says them nay;
        For, be't in pulpit or in street,
        'Tis most unwise to ask if they
        Be men to whom revenge is sweet.

CX   Item, I leave to Friar Baude
        (Of Carmelitish habitance:
        His countenance is bold and broad)
        A sallet and two partisans,
        Lest Tusca[91] and his ruffians
        Should seek to rob his pretty cage.[92]
        Though old, he'll set them all a dance;
        He is a devil when in rage.

82

CXI Item, whereas the learned Sealer[93]
     So much of flyshit[94] hath to chew,
     I leave him, as an honest dealer,
     A gob of spittle to bedew
     His seal, that it may render true,
     And make an imprint round and fair.
     (I mean the Bishop's seal, mark you!
     For of the rest may God take care.)

CXII Item, my Lords the Auditors[95]
      Shall have that barn of theirs new-lin'd,
      And infants' chairs, to ease the sores
      That plague so many a behind;
      But only if they bear in mind
      That Macée[96] of Orleans, the wench
      Who stole my purse, be smartly fin'd,
      For she's an evil little stench.

CXIII Item, I leave a gaud to deck
       Sweet Master Francis Vacquerie —[97]
       A high Scots gorget for his neck,[98] [100]
       Devoid of gold or jewelry;
       For when he stood in pillory[99]
       He swore by God and by Saint George.[100]
       No man who hears that history
       Can help but laugh with all his gorge.

CXIV Item, to luckless Master Laurens,[101]
      Whose eyes are always red, poor chap,
      (A curse he herits from his parents,
      Who drank their wine straight from the tap),
      I leave the lining of my cap,
      To wipe away their rheumy milk.
      Were he John Cœur,[102] why, then, mayhap,
      He'd purge his eyes on purest silk.

CXV   Item, to Master John Cotart
I owe a farthing, I surmise,
As fee for having ta'en my part
As counsel at the Church Assize
When I was cited by Denise[103]
On a false charge of calumny.
To help his soul, that it may rise
To Heav'n, I wrote this litany:

BALLADE

OLD Father Noah, who didst plant the vine;
And Lot, who didst carouse so lustily
That Love, who all men's wits doth undermine,
Caus'd thee with thine own daughters twain to lie
(I utter not these words in obloquy;)
Architricline,[104] who knowest well this art;
I beg you all, of your sweet clemency,
Pray for the soul of Master John Cotart!

He was a proper scion of your line,
He who would drink the best that cash could buy,
Though afterwards he knew not where to dine.
The flow'r of all our tosspot chivalry
Was he – a title no man will deny.
He drank and drank, with an unwearied heart.
Great Lords, do not refuse your ministry.
Pray for the soul of Master John Cotart!

Oft have I seen him wend his serpentine
Way home to bed, feet stumbling all awry;
And I remember how he black'd his eyne
In an encounter with a butchery.

84

You might explore the world ere you'ld espy
A man so nimble with a pint or quart.
Ah, when at Heaven's Gate you hear him cry,
Pray for the soul of Master John Cotart!

Prince, he could scarcely spit, he was so dry;
He'ld moan: 'My gullet hath a burning smart!'
Nothing could slake that vast aridity.
Pray for the soul of Master John Cotart!

CXVI   Item, I bid that Marle,[105] the younger,
    (Since money plagues me like a murrain)
    Be my official moneymonger;
    Provided that, in ev'ry bargain
    With vendors either French or foreign,
    For each gold crown he give two pence,
    And for each pound at least a florin:
    Lovers must not begrudge expense.

CXVII   Item, upon my pilgrimage
    I heard that my three orphan'd souls[106]
    Are thriving, and are nigh of age.
    They study hard, obey all rules;
    There's not a child in all the schools
    More skill'd than these at casting sums.
    Now, by the Order of All Fools,[107]
    Such children are no suck-a-thumbs!

CXVIII Let them be therefore sent to College:
    Where? Peter Richier's[108] is the place!
    Donat's[109] beyond their pow'rs of knowledge;
    I do not seek to force their pace.
    Let them but learn a simple grace,
    Ave salus, tibi decus,[110]
    And therewith be content: the race
    Is seldom to the studious.

CXIX   'Tis enough Latin for their need.
        When they have learnt it, then, heave-to!
        Let them not study the long Creed;
        For children 'tis too much ado.
        I split my tabard into two,
        And let the half of it be sold
        To buy them a cream-tart or so:
        Sweets never leave young people cold.

CXX   And let them learn polite discourse,
        Whatever it may cost in slaps,
        With thumbs held firmly on the purse
        And hoods drawn down about their chaps.
        Let them be taught to doff their caps
        And say: 'How now? Fellow, good-den!'
        Then all the world will say, perhaps:
        'What well-bred little gentlemen!'

CXXI   Item, those poor and needy clerks[111]
        To whom my titles I resign'd,
        Fine youngsters and as gay as larks
        (It was their beauty took my mind,
        When I so lavishly assign'd,
        Asking no guaranty at all,
        The rent, as from a date consign'd,
        Of William Gueuldry's butcher-stall),[111]

CXXII   Yes, I applaud and love them still,
        Despite their youthful insolence.
        In forty years, if God so will,
        They'll show a mighty difference.
        Whoever causes them offence,
        Or seeks to strike them now and then,
        Is but a churl and lacking sense,
        For children in good time grow men.

CXXIII   The scholarships of The Eighteen[112]
They'll have: this charge I'll undertake.[112]
No dormice, they, to close their eyne
Three months on end ere they awake.
For, sure, it is a sad mistake
To spend your youthtime in a doze,
And then be forc'd to watch and wake
In age, when most you need repose.

CXXIV   I've told the Keeper of the Roll
What he must do in this affair.
So let these lads pray for my soul,
Or earn a buffet on the ear.
It causes tongues to wag, I fear,
That I to them so much incline;
But, by my Patron Saint I swear,
Their mothers were no friends of mine!

CXXV   Item to Culdoe,[113] who shall share
The gift with Messire Charles Taranna,[114]
I leave five shillings ('Gotten where?'
Let them not ask: 'twill come like manna,
'Midst exclamations of Hosanna);
Also my boots of good sheep's leather,[115]
To give my greetings to Joanna[116]
And other birds of the same feather.

CXXVI   Item, unto the Lord of Grigny,
To whom I left Bicêtre before,[117]
I now bequeath the tower of Billy,[118]
Provided that, if any door
Or pane be broken, he'll restore
The whole, nor ever call on me
To help him pay the woundy score:
I have no money, nor has he.

CXXVII Item, to Tybalt de la Garde . . .
Tybalt? I lie, his name is John,[119]
(Which trifle can I best discard?
Grave losses have I lately known:
May God make restitution!)
I'll give him – yes, 'The Cask', I think,
Though Master Genevoys,[120] I'll own,
Is older and more vers'd in drink.

CXXVIII Item, I leave to Basennier,[121]
Court clerk and notary, a creel
Of cloves, the which he may require
Of worthy Master John Ruel.[122]
The same to Mautaint[121] and Rosnel;[123]
And I command them to defer,
In vassalage and service leal,
To him who serves Saint Christopher.[124]

CXXIX For him I've written this ballade
To her whom all men idolize,
His lady wife. If he hath had
More luck than most, 'tis no surprise,
For he did win her as a prize
One day in good King René's lists.[125]
Like Troy's great knights, in this emprise
His tongue was tied, but not his fists.[126]

BALLADE

A T daybreak, when the falcon 'gins to bate,
M oved thereunto by noble wantonness
(*B* etimes the merry thrushes flit and prate!),
R eceives his breakfast, settling with address

O ver the lure, such joyance and largesse
I offer thee as lovers long to get.
S weet Cupid wrote it in his book, express:
E 'en for this end thou, love, and I are met.

D earest, o'er all my heart shalt rule in state,
E nthron'd, until I pass to nothingness,
L aurel who art the champion of my fate,
O live who dost assuage all bitterness.
R eason not only bids I never cease
E nserving thee (which is my loving debt),
But that my servitude shall aye increase:
E'en for this end thou, love, and I are met.

Nay, more, when I am sad and desolate,
And scowling Fortune doth me most oppress,
Thy gentle glance can chase away her hate,
Like feather 'neath a zephyr's mild caress.
The seed I sow in thee is none the less
Mine own, if mine own likeness it beget.
God bids I till and give thee fruitfulness:
E'en for this end thou, love, and I are met.

Princess, hear now the faith which I profess:
Thy heart and mine shall nevermore be set
Asunder; and thou wilt the same confess:
E'en for this end thou, love, and I are met.

CXXX   Item, I leave to John Perdrier[127]
        And Francis,[128] who's the younger son,
        Nothing: 'twas ever their desire
        To share their wealth with me. (I own

89

That Frank, that child of malison,
Most kindly once my cause did urge
In a long screed, half sneer, half moan,
That stood me in good stead at Bourges.[129]

CXXXI His tongue's so hot that I consulted
Taillevent's[130] chapter on ragouts.
But of that labour naught resulted;
He nowhere tells of such a sauce.
Nay, it was Saint Macarius
(Who cook'd the Devil hair and hide
And found the smell most savorous)
Who this receipt of mine supplied.

BALLADE

In arsenic, realgar triturate;
In quicklime and saltpetre; in a froth
Of boiling lead, where let them macerate;
In soot and pitch left soaking in a broth
Of urine from a ghetto's public booth;
In rinsings from a leper's mangy poll;
In scrapings from a patten's crusted sole;
In philtres venomous; in viper's blood;
In gall of fox and wolf and eldritch owl,
Let all such envious tongues as these be stew'd!

In brains of an old hydrophobic cat,
Grimalkin who hath neither claw nor tooth,
Or of a mastiff so infuriate
That slobber overflows his baying mouth;
In flecks of spume, congeal'd by dust and drouth

Upon the flanks of a wind-broken mule;
In water where the rat hath dipp'd its jowl,
Together with the slimy snake and toad,
Lizard and frog and other noble fowl,
Let all such envious tongues as these be stew'd!

In dangerous corrosive sublimate;
In navel torn from serpent still in youth;
In blood left drying on a surgeon's plate
When a full moon ascends the azimuth
(Blood either black, or green as leeks, or both);
In chancres and in ulcers; in a bowl
Wherein a nurse has wash'd her baby's tow'l;
In basin where a trull has shed her load
(He whom this puzzles is a simple soul),
Let all such envious tongues as these be stew'd!

Prince, take this dainty dish and sift the whole
(If you have neither sieve nor sack nor shroud)
Through dirty draw'rs with grease and sweat
    imbued;
But, first, in a fat porker's filthy stool
Let all such envious tongues as these be stew'd!

CXXXII   Item, to Couraud,[131] as is right,
I leave *Frank Goutier's Refutation*.[132]
As for 'the tyrant in his might',[133]
To him I make no supplication.
A weary man of humble station,
I heed the Preacher's words: 'Beware
Of causing mighty men vexation,
Lest they entice thee in a snare.'

CXXXIII Gontier himself I do not fear,[134]
For he hath no more means than I,
And no retainers at his rear.
Yet he doth praise his poverty
(As who should praise calamity!)
And doth for happiness repute
That which I count as misery.
Let's take the matter to dispute.

BALLADE

(*The Refutation of Frank Gontier*)[135]

A PORTLY canon lolls on taffeta,
Close by a stove, in chamber well appointed,
And at his side the Dame Sidonia,
Smooth, tender, white and pleasantly anointed.
They quaff their hippocras[136] in stoups uncounted
And laugh and sport and dally all the day,
Stark naked both, to speed their am'rous play.
Through mortise-chink I saw them hug and squeeze,
And then I knew, to chase dull care away
There is no treasure like a life of ease.

If Gontier and his sweetheart Helena
Had ever been with such delights acquainted,
They'ld leave their onions, leeks *et cetera* –
No fare for those who love a breath untainted.
Their buttermilk and broth, so highly vaunted,
Are not a fico worth, in my assay.
What if they couch together 'neath the may?
Is it not better far to warm the knees
'Twixt linen sheets? What is your answer, pray?
There is no treasure like a life of ease.

They make their merry Saturnalia
With water and coarse barley-bread unstinted.
Not all the birds from here to Africa[137]
Could hold me for a single hour contented
With such a rural scene as these frequented.
Well, in God's name, let them make holiday,
Lover and lass, beneath the briar gay:
I gladly leave them to their jollities.
But, be the shepherd's blisses what they may,
There is no treasure like a life of ease.

Prince, be our judge, this cause of ours to weigh.
Let me but add (I seek not to displease),
Whilst yet a babe I often heard men say:
There is no treasure like a life of ease.

CXXXIV   Item, because her Bible knowledge
Gives Dame Bruyères[138] the right to teach,
I bid that she and all her college
Of damsels do go forth and preach
The Gospels unto girls whose speech
Is grown a little free and rough;
But not in graveyards,[139] I beseech –
The Halls[140] will serve them well enough.

BALLADE

(Ballade of the women of Paris)

THOUGH other women put on airs,
Florentines and Venetians,
Because they're glib to sell their wares,
Even when old; though Paduans

And Romans and Lombardians
And Piedmontese can sing a song,
Likewise the Alessandrians,
'Tis Paris hath the ready tongue.

'Tis said that girls hold public chairs
Amongst the Neapolitans;
And German women prate like stares,
Both Prussians and Bavarians.
But be they Greeks, Egyptians,
Whatever coasts you seek along,
Spaniards or Catalonians,
'Tis Paris hath the ready tongue.

Bretons are dumb in most affairs,
Gascons make little utterance.
Two fishwives from our thoroughfares
Would quickly leave them all mumchance –
The English, the Calaisians
(My list is growing over-long),
The Picards, the Valencians:
'Tis Paris hath the ready tongue.

Prince, to our fair Parisians
Award the prize that doth belong:
Let others vaunt th' Italians,
'Tis Paris hath the ready tongue.

CXXXV Behold these dames, in twos or threes,
  Crouch'd on the kirtle's lowest hem
  In churches or in monast'ries.
  Silently creep up close to them;

You'll find that ev'ry apophthegm
Outdoes Macrobius for discerning.
Give heed, and you may steal a gem,
For these are lessons well worth learning.

CXXXVI Item, unto that ancient keep,
Montmartre, which now is barr'd to man,[141]
I do adjoin that stony heap
Ycleped Mount Valerian;[142]
I give it, furthermore, a span
Of my indulgence brought from Rome:
Thus many a good Christian
Shall here find spiritual home.

CXXXVII Item, let there be revelry
Amongst the servants of the great,
With cakes and tarts and minstrelsy
And dancing till the hour is late.
Why stop at seven pints or eight
When lord and lady are asleep?
Then let the hubbub swift abate
As off to am'rous joys they creep.

CXXXVIII Item, young maids of high degree,
With aunts and parents to observe them,
I' faith, they shall have naught from me;
I've given all to those who serve them.
Yet such a little would preserve them
From utter woe, these maidens rich
Who've let Dominicans disserve them,
And now are plagu'd by hunger's itch!

CXXXIX   Aye, all these friars, of ev'ry Order,
Although their lives are strict and stern,
Have a right plenty in their larder
Of that for which poor maidens yearn;
As Jacqueline doth well discern,
Or Isabel who cries: 'I' fecks!'
A man will scarce deserve to burn
For ministering to their lacks.

CXL   Item, I leave unto Fat Margie[143]
A face that's fair in ev'ry feature.
As I'm a member of the clergy
(She, too, is a God-fearing creature),
I love her in my deepest nature,
And she loves me, the darling toad.
If any meet her peradventure,
Let him recite her this ballade:

BALLADE

(The ballade of Fat Margie)[144]

IF I do serve my love with all my heart,
Must you, then, take me for a rogue or sot?
For certain charms she hath no counterpart.
With her I am a very Lancelot:
When people come, I run to drink a pot,
I 'go for wine' with soft and nimble tread,
I fetch them water, cheese and fruit and bread,
If they pay well, I cry them: '*Bene stat*;
Pray come again, when you've a load to shed,
To this bordèl where we are thron'd in state!'

But afterwards a bitter brawl may start,
When Margie comes back home without a groat.
Then hatred of her stabs me like a dart;
I seize her gown, her girdle and her coat
And swear I'll sell them all to pay her scot;
Whereat she screams, with arms akimbo spread,
And swears, by all the living and the dead,
It shall not be! And then I seize a slat
And score her face with notches fiery red,
In this bordèl where we are thron'd in state.

Then peace is made and she lets flee a fart,
Like an envenom'd beetle all a-bloat,
And lays her hand upon my privy part.
'Go, go!'[145] she cries, and smites my tender spot.
Both drunk, we slumber like a worn-out boot.
At dawn her rumbling stomach wakes her greed;
She mounts me, eager not to waste my seed.
I groan beneath her, flatten'd by her weight,
Until the very life of me is sped,
In this bordèl where we are thron'd in state.

Come wind, come hail, come frost, I've bak'd my
    bread.[146]
A lecher to a lecheress is wed.
Which is the worse? There's little to be said.
Like unto like: 'Bad cat for a bad rat.'
We love the mire, and miry is our bed;
We flee from honour, honour now is fled,[147]
In this bordèl where we are thron'd in state.

CXLI   Item, to Marion l'Ydolle
        And to big Jenny of Britaine
        I leave the right to found a school
        At which the pupils wield the cane –

A practice that doth much obtain,
Though not within the gaol of Meun.
'Twill need no door-sign to explain
What sort of study there goes on.

CXLII   Item, I leave a sheaf of switches,
In my own garden freshly grown,
To false Noël,[148] to warm his breeches.
Chastisement is a handsome boon,
And none should seek to be immune.
I leave him ten score lashes, all
Applied in the same afternoon
By worthy Master Hangman Hal.[149]

CXLIII   Item, I know not what bequest
On the alms-houses to bestow.
This is no time nor place for jest;
The poor have miseries enow.
Men send them bones, too well I know.
The Mendicants have had my goose:
Well, to the poor the bones must go:
'Small men, small needs' be my excuse.

CXLIV   Item, I leave unto my barber,
Colin, whose surname is Galerne
(The druggist Angelot's his neighbour),
A cake of ice fetch'd from the Marne,
To serve as poultice. Let him burn
His belly with it night and day,
So that, when summer shall return,
He may be warm, beneath the clay.

CXLV   Item, unto the Foundlings, naught;
The Lostlings,[150] though, I must console.
They can be found if they are sought
In care of Marion l'Ydolle.[151]

They'll have instruction at my school.
'Tis brief, so let them all be seated
And hearken well, nor play the fool.
This lesson will not be repeated.

GOOD ADVICE TO LOST SHEEP

'FAIR children, you will surely grieve
To lose your fairest rose of all,
Young clerks who learn to pick and thieve;
For if you go to Sharpers' Hall [152]
Or Robbers' Inn,[152] beware a fall!
Do not frequent such evil nooks,
Nor trust the worth of an appeal:[153]
Thus perish'd Colin of Cayeux.[154]

'Think not of making reparation
For this is no three-farthing game:
You risk your neck and your salvation;
And he who loses dies in shame,
And he who wins gets no great name,
Nor Punic Dido for a wife.
That man's a fool and much to blame
Who for so little stakes his life

'They say, and 'tis a truth, alack!
'Gainst which 'twere folly to contend,
That e'en a waggonload of sack
Is empty by the summer's end.
Your booty earns no dividend,
'Tis soon and quickly spent again.
Whose fortunes do ye think to mend?
Ill-gotten riches are no gain.'

BALLADE

(*Ballade of Good Doctrine*)

WHETHER you choose to carry bulls,[155]
To cog the dice, or to purvey
False coin, 'tis all a game for gulls:
You'll burn your fingers, one fine day,
Like men who perjure and betray.[156]
Whether you lag or prig or chouse,
Where do your profits run away?
All to the taverns and the stews.

Rhyme or lampoon, turn motley fools,[157]
With drums and flutes and cymbals gay,
Rattle your quips, or stand on stools
By showmen's booths to bawl and bray;
Travel with mime or Passion-play;
At gleek or ninepins take your dues:
You'll throw the winnings – hearken, pray! –
All to the taverns and the stews.

If for such filth your passion cools,
Go till the fields and ted the hay;
Go serve as chambermaid to mules
If you can find no better lay.
Hunger, at worst, you'll hold at bay.
But even if you pick and bruise
Harsh oakum, won't you take your pay
All to the taverns and the stews?

Pack up your gear and fine array,
Your corded doublets, hats and hose,
And bear them off, without delay,
All to the taverns and the stews.

CXLVI   To you, companions in debauch
         That charms the flesh and kills the sprite,
         I say, perpend the sooty smirch
         That turns dead bodies black as night.
         Beware, it hath an evil bite;
         Flee and escape it while you may;
         And bear in mind, in Hell's despite,
         That each of you must die one day.

CXLVII   Item, I leave the Fifteen Score,[158]
         That ill-provided multitude
         Of blind, to whom I ever bore
         A certain debt of gratitude,
         My spectacles, to make them shrewd
         Of vision, that they may discern
         Betwixt the wicked and the good
         When at the Innocents[159] they mourn.

CXLVIII They do not jest nor laugh, these dead!
         What comes of great inheritance,
         Or sporting in a stately bed,
         Or drinking wine with wagging paunch,
         Or jollity, or feast, or dance,
         Or readiness for any game?
         Such joys have no perpetuance,
         And naught remaineth but the blame.

CXLIX   When I consider all the skulls
         Deep in these vaults together squeez'd,
         They all were Masters of Appeals,
         Or City Treasurers, at least;
         Or maybe all these poor deceas'd
         Were market-porters – who can tell?
         Lamplighter, bishop, lay or priest,
         They're all alike, where now they dwell.

CL And all those other skulls, that bow'd
One to another, in their day,
Some condescending, high and proud,
And others stooping to obey,
They give no greeting now, perfay!
Assembled in a nameless muster.
Their lordships have been reft away:
Which is the scribe, and which the master?

CLI They're dead, God rest their souls, amen!
Their flesh is tatter'd to a shred,
E'en though they once were noblemen
Or noble ladies, softly bred,
On creams and cakes and tartlets fed,
Their bones are moulder'd unto dust
Whence joy and merriment are fled:
In Jesus let them put their trust!

CLII This is my final benediction
Both on the dead and on the quick –
On all who sit in jurisdiction,
In court, assize or bailiwick,
Who for the body politic
Have worn their bodies to a shade:
May God and sweet Saint Dominic[160]
Absolve them all, when they are dead!

CLIII Item, I've nothing for James Cardon[161]
Worth his acceptance – I regret
Such poverty, and beg his pardon –
Except this little *bergeronnette*:[162]
Sung to the tune of *Marionette*
(Written for Marion Peautarde)
Or *Open, open Guillemette*,
It might some merriment afford.

DITTY

On my return from that harsh prison
Where I left all but life behind,
If Fortune yet doth prove unkind,
How great, alas, is her misprision!
Methinks that now she hath good reason
To be appeas'd and change her mind,
On my return!

But if her fury hath no season
And still she rageth unconfin'd,
Please God my ransom'd soul may find
A refuge in His Heav'nly mansion,
On my return!

CLIV   Item, I leave to Master Lomer[163]
(As fairy child, I have his right)
The pow'r to lie with ev'ry comer.
But, since it is but small delight
To lie with whores, the lucky wight
Shall nothing pay, nor need abstain
From coupling ninety times a night –
A fig for Ogier the Dane![164]

CLV   Item, to ev'ry heartsick lover
(I'll spare him Master Alan Chartier)[165]
I leave a font that's brimming over
With tears in place of holy water,
Likewise a sprig of briar, the better
The drops amongst the crowd to dole,
Provided he recite a psalter
For Francis Villon's wretched soul.

CLVI   Item, let Master Jamie James,[166]
Who toils for riches, offer vows
Of marriage unto many dames,
But ne'er an one of them espouse,
He drudges but for his own house,
And finds the least disbursement bitter:
'Tis plain that what was once the sow's
Belongeth rightly to the litter.[167]

CLVII   Item, that noble Seneschal[168]
Who did so much my lot to ease,
Shall hold the rank of mareschal,[169]
As farrier to ducks and geese.
I send him this poor, trifling piece
To take his mind from his distress.
'Twill serve as kindling, an he please:
Much reading breeds much weariness.

CLVIII   Item, the Captain of the Guard
Shall have two pretty little pages,[170]
Big Marquet and young Philibart,[171]
Good lads, keen-witted for their ages,
As Tristan Th'Eremite[171] engages,
Whom they have serv'd for many a year;
But now, alas! for lack of wages
They'll soon go barefoot, much I fear.

CLIX   Item, to Chappelain[172] shall pass
My right of simple chaplaincy,
To say unconsecrated mass,
Which needs no great Latinity.
He could have had my curacy,[173]
But such preferment he evades;
He finds confessions dull and dry,
Save those of mistresses and maids.

CLX Item, good Master John of Calais,[174]
Who is a man of honest fame
And doth not bear me any malice
(He doth not even know my name),
As arbiter I do proclaim,
And hereby fully authorize
To judge of ev'ry rival claim,
However small, that may arise:

CLXI With gloss and nearer definition,
With commentary and prescription,
With diminution and addition,
Ratification and prescription;
Or, if time lacketh for transcription,
With word-of-mouth arbitrament,
According to his best conception:
To all of this I give consent.

CLXII And if some heir, whilst I did journey,
Hath left this life here for a better,
John Calais shall, as my attorney,
Amend and regulate the matter,
And that bequest, by deed of letter,
Unto some other heir enlarge,
Nor be thereof his own resetter:[175]
Upon his soul I lay this charge.

CLXIII Item, I bid that Saint Avoye
Shall be the place where I am laid.[176]
That all men may behold with joy
My beauty, let me be portray'd
In fullest likeness, foot to head –
In ink, unless the cost be great.
Of monument I have no need:
The floor would burst beneath its weight.[176]

CLXIV   Item, I bid that round my grave
These words be writ, for all to read,
In letters eloquent and brave
(If ink be lacking, write, instead,
In charcoal or perchance in lead,
But so as not to hurt the plaster:
That men may say, when I am dead,
'He was a mad but merry roister'.):

CLXV   E P I T A P H

HERE IN THIS UPPER ROOM[177] IS LAIN
POOR FRANCIS VILLON, DEEP AT REST:
A LITTLE SCHOLAR WHO WAS SLAIN
BY CUPID'S FATAL ARBALEST.
HE NE'ER A ROOD OF LAND POSSESS'D,
BUT GAVE AWAY ALL HE DID OWN,
TABLE AND BENCH, CUPBOARD AND CHEST.
LOVERS, RECITE THIS ORISON:

P R A Y E R

LORD, grant him everlasting rest,
And with Thy light his darkness heal.
So poor he was, with ne'er a skeel
Nor dish nor sprig of parsley blest.
His head and eyebrows, chin and chest
Were hairless as an onion-peel.
Lord, grant him everlasting rest.

The law's harsh rigour him oppress'd,
And with a shovel smote his keel,
What though he clamour'd: 'I appeal!'[178] –
Scarce an ambiguous request.
Lord, grant him everlasting rest.

106

CLXVI   Item, I wish that a wild peal
Be rung from Notre-Dame's great bell.
'Tis made of glass,[179] yet hearts congeal
To hear its dreadful clangour swell.
It oft hath serv'd the nation well
And saved full many a house from plunder.
Its warning clarion can repel
An hostile army, aye, or thunder.

CLXVII   The ringers of this mighty bell
Shall have four loaves; nay, they shall even
Have six, if need be. (Sooth to tell,
I mean such loaves as had Saint Stephen.)[180]
Volant's[181] a man of valour proven:
He shall be one: and his reward
Will nourish him six days or seven.
The other? Who but John la Garde?[182]

CLXVIII   To carry out this Testament
I do appoint as counsellors
Six men with whom I'm well content,
Modest and rev'rend seniors
Who satisfy their creditors,
And are, praise God! of good estate.
Let these be my executors:
Set down their names as I dictate.

CLXIX   There's Master Martin Bellefaye,[183]
Who in Crown causes doth excel.
Who'll be the second? Let me weigh
The thing . . . I've hit it, all is well!
Good Messire William Colombel[184]
Shall take this charge, if he consent.
The third? Why, Michael Jouvenel![185]
These three shall be plenipotent.

CLXX   But if they seek to make excuse,
Lest the first costs should be too great,
Or if they utterly refuse,
In place of them I designate
Three pillars of the Church and State,[186]
Philip Brunel, a noble squire,[186]
And, as his next associate,
His neighbour, Master James Raguier.[186]

CLXXI   And, thirdly, Master Jamie James:[186]
Three men of worth and reputation,
God-fearing, mindful of the flames
Of Hell and eager for salvation.
Rather than break this obligation,
They'ld gladly spend of their own treasure.
They shall have sole administration
And carve the sirloin at their pleasure.

CLXXII   The so-called Master of Probate [187]
Shall have no tittle nor no jot,
Saving that young Licentiate
Of Arts whose name is Tom Tricot.[188]
I'ld gladly drink upon his scot;
And, if he play'd a better role
At tennis,[189] I would cavil not
To leave him Mistress Perrette's Hole.[190]

CLXXIII   Concerning candles for my soul,
William Du Ru[191] shall furnish these.
To hold the tassels of my pall
I designate my six trustees.
I feel my stabbing pains increase;
Beard, scalp and eyebrows itch and gall.
'Tis time for me to make my peace
And cry gramercy to men all.

BALLADE

To Mendicants, Carthusians,
Celestines and all Devotees,
To idlers and Corinthians,
To market-porters and bargees,
To maids in narrow bodices,
To little fops, in Cupid's thrall,
Whose boots are tight around the knees,
I cry gramercy to them all.

To girls who show extravagance
Of bosom, in desire to tease,
To revellers who shout and dance,
To men with monkeys full of fleas,
To all who clown or carol glees
Or jostle in the streets and bawl,
To Jennifers and Jessamies,
I cry gramercy to them all,

Saving those filthy ruffians,
The mastiffs of the Town police,
Who made me gnaw such evil scrans.[192]
Henceforth I'll have no fear of these:
Into their snouts I'ld fart or sneeze,
But cannot, for in bed I sprawl.
So, as a man who loveth peace,
I cry gramercy to them all.

Prince, take the pack of them, and grease
Their costards with a massive maul
Or loaded club or spiked mace.
I cry gramercy to them all.

ANOTHER BALLADE

HERE ends the Will and Testament
Of that poor fellow, Francis Villon.
Come to his grave and make lament,
When you shall hear the bells' quadrilion,[193]
Clad all in garments of vermilion;
For Love it was his life did reave.
To this he swore by old Apollyon
When of this world he begg'd his leave.

I think his words were truly meant:
His mistress used him like a scullion
And drove him into banishment,
So that from Paris to Rousillon
There was no sprig of thyme nor saffron
(He said, and sought not to deceive)
But bore a tatter of his apron
When of this world he begg'd his leave.

Aye, when he took the sacrament
He'd but one rag upon his quarron.[194]
Nay, more, Love did not then relent,
But smote him with an harpy's talon
And spear'd him like a leaping salmon.
So strange a thing you'ld scarce believe,
That Love could be so foul a felon
When of this world he begg'd his leave.

Prince, who art noble as a falcon,
Hear what he did on that last eve,
He drank a swig of red Morillon
When of this world he begg'd his leave.

VILLON'S EPITAPH[1]

MEN, brothers whom we shall not see again,
Let not your hearts towards us be unkind;
For if you pity us poor men and plain,
God's mercy unto you will be inclin'd.
Here you behold some six of us alin'd.
Our flesh, that we did all too well supply,
Did long since shrivel up and putrefy,
And we, the bones, to dust and ashes fall.
Let none make sport of our adversity,
But pray to God that he forgive us all!

We call you brothers. Nay, do not disdain
The kinship, though it was by seal'd and sign'd
Mandate of law that we poor six were slain:
Not all men always are of righteous mind.
Now we are dead, we've left our sins behind;
So plead with Jesus that his charity
Towards us erring sheep may not run dry,
But save us from the flame perpetual.
We're dead, no soul torments us inwardly;
But pray to God that he forgive us all!

We have been wash'd and purified by rain;
The sun hath burnt us to a blacken'd rind;
The crows and magpies have dug out our eyen;
Eyebrows and beard are from our faces twin'd.
We have no rest: always the changing wind

Hunteth us to and fro, now low, now high.
Our skins are pitted like a strawberry
Where birds have peck'd them. Ye who would
                                        forestall
Such vengeance, be not of our company,
But pray to God that he forgive us all!

Jesus, who over all hast mastery,
Guard us from Satan's wicked signory:
He hath no rightful claim on us nor call.
Mankind, this is no place for mockery;
But pray to God that he forgive us all!

JE SUIS FRANÇOIS[1]...

❧

FRANCIS by name, France's by birth
(I've never had much luck on earth),
At Paris first I op'd my eyes
(It is a hamlet near Pontoise);[2]
And soon my neck, to end the farce,
Must learn how heavy is my arse.[3]

QUESTION ASKED OF THE
GAOL-CLERK

~∞~

WHAT think you now of my appeal,[1]
   Garnier?[2] Was that mere vanity?
Nay, ev'ry beast in pain will squeal;
If any seek its limbs to tie,
'Twill battle for its liberty
And when you sought to prejudice
My purpose with yon homily,[2]
Was that a time to hold my peace?

Had I been kin to Hugh Capel,
That scion of a butchery,[3]
I'ld ne'er have drunk so great a deal
Of water[4] in their tannery[5]
(You know the tricks of coggery?)[6]
But when, by that foul artifice,[4]
I fell beneath their tyranny,
Was that a time to hold my peace?

Thought you that 'twixt my head and heel
Was not enough philosophy
To find the words for: 'I appeal!'?
Aye, aye, there was, I certify;
My wits are scarce, but not awry.
When, in full court, I heard that voice:
'Thou shalt be hang'd!' pray testify,
Was that a time to hold my peace?

114

Prince, if the pip had hush'd my cry,
I'ld be today in Clotaire's place,
Strung in the meadows like a spy:
Was that a time to hold my peace?

IN PRAISE OF THE COURT[1]

(*Petition to the Lords of Parliament*)

⟡

A L L my five senses, ear and mouth and eye,
My nose, and likewise thou, my sense of touch;
All ye my members black with infamy,
Make utterance in his own fashion each:
'Most sov'reign Court, when we were left in lurch,
You sav'd us from our wretchedness and fear.
The tongue alone will not suffice to bear
To you full token of our gratitude;
Wherefore we all in this thanksgiving share,
Sister of Angels, mother of the good!'

Heart, rend thyself in twain, or liquefy;
Be not more obdurate or hard to broach
Than was that great brown rock on Sinai
Which did to Israel repentance teach.
My tears, gush forth, in thankfulness approach,
Like a poor, contrite soul freed from despair;
Praise ye the Court, that succour brings and cheer
To France and men of other nationhood,
That offspring whom sweet Heav'n herself did bear,
Sister of Angels, mother of the good!'

And ye, my teeth, let each one sev'rally
Forth from my mouth in ecstasy debouch;
Louder than organ, trump or bell give cry,
And have no care to eat. Nay, inasmuch
As death but lately had me in its clutch,

116

IN PRAISE OF THE COURT

Do you, my lungs, who still draw in the air,
And you, my body, viler than a bear,
Worse than a pig that makes its nest in mud,
Praise ye the Court, whilst yet ye humbly dare,
Sister of Angels, mother of the good!

Prince, but three days permit me tarry here,
To bid farewell to those I hold most dear.
Without their aid I have no coin for food.
Triumphant Court, do not refuse my prayer,
Sister of Angels, mother of the good!

NOTES

NOTES

TRANSLATOR'S FOREWORD

[1] Poems not translated: 'Ballade of Proverbs'; 'Ballade of Small Matters'; 'Ballade of Paradoxes'; 'Rondeau (Jenin l'Avenue)'; 'Epistle to Marie of Orleans'; 'Ballade spoken by Fortune'; and seven ballades in Jargon.

BALLADE OF GOOD COUNSEL

[1] L.T. describes this poem as 'beginner's work', and comments: 'This ballade, which, whatever may be said, is very mediocre, nevertheless has a certain interest for the moral biography of the poet at a period when he was still an honest man, or, rather, had not yet broken with all feeling for honesty. . . .'

[2] In the original, the first six lines of this Envoy form an acrostic, their initial letters spelling the word 'Villon'.

THE BEQUESTS

Most editors have entitled Villon's two long poems *The Little Testament* and *The Great Testament*. I prefer to entitle them *The Bequests* and *The Testament*, since Villon himself, in stanza LXV of the latter poem, declares that the former had been called a 'Testament' without his consent.

[2] L.T. quotes from Vegetius' *De re militari*: 'The ancients had the custom of setting down in writing those things that they deemed good to know, and made books of them, which books they offered to princes.'

[3] In a single night, in September 1438, fourteen grown people were killed and eaten by wolves between Montmartre and the Porte St. Antoine. (C.M.)

[4] Katherine de Vausselles, believed by A.L. to have been a niece and house-companion of Maître Pierre du Vaucel, a canon of Saint-Benoît-le-Bientourné, where Maître Guillaume de Villon, François's foster-father, was a chaplain. If this is so, she was a close neighbour of the poet. He loved her vainly for many years. Cf. *The Testament*, 'Double Ballade' following stanza LIV, and the relevant notes.

[5] Nothing is known of the wrong, if any, that she did to Villon, unless this passage refers to the incident mentioned in the above 'Double Ballade'.

[6] In the original *ils ont vers moi les piez blans*: no toll was paid on horses with four white feet. (L.T.)

[7] It is possible that Villon had either or both of two other reasons for visiting Angers (if he, indeed, did so): (1) To plan a burglary from, or to sponge on, a monk living there, who was his maternal uncle; cf. *The Testament*, LXXVIII, note 2. (2) To present a letter of introduction to the court of King René of Sicily, who was temporarily in residence there; cf. note to *The Testament*, LXXXII. (L.T.)

[8] A sardonically magniloquent expression, borrowed from its contemporary use in descriptions of the estates of princes and noblemen. (L.T.)

[9] Marchant was the son of a wealthy councillor of Parliament; Cornu was a financier. They had presumably lent Villon money. (L.T.)

[10] Pierre Saint-Amand, a fiscal officer. Such officers commonly rode on white horses or mules. Villon leaves him two appropriately named taverns. (L.T.) C.M. describes Saint-Amand as a wealthy financier. Cf. note 56 to *The Testament*, LXXXVII.

[11] A goldsmith. (L.T.)

[12] Diamond.

[13] The original contains a joke the point of which is not known. (L.T.)

[14] In 1209 the Lateran Council bade all Christians confess at least once a year to their parish priests. In 1409, however, a Bull issued by Nicholas V gave mendicant friars the right to hear confessions—to the annoyance of the University and bishops of France, who, at about the time when Villon was writing *The Bequests*, persuaded Calixtus III to revoke this Bull. (L.T.)

[15] Robert Vallée, a wealthy man. (L.T.)

[16] Johanne de Millières, Vallée's mistress, was noted for her domineering nature. (L.T.)

[17] *L'Art de Memoire*, a school-book. (L.T.)

[18] The church of Saint-Jacques-la-Boucherie. (L.T.)

[19] Jacques Cardon, a rich draper. (L.T.) Cf. *The Testament*, CLIII.

[20] i.e. nothing at all. L.T. also reads into this phrase a joking reference to Cardon's porcine plumpness.

[21] A friend and neighbour of Villon, and about two years older than the poet. He was a man of noble family who had fallen into evil ways. In 1452 he had been arrested by two sergeants whom he had assaulted outside a tavern known as *la Grosse Margot* (Cf. *The Testament*, CXL and following Ballade), and had been banished from Paris. After committing a number of burglaries (including some sacrilegious thefts), he was hanged in 1457. (A.L.)

[22] Only noblemen were allowed to keep hunting dogs. (L.T.)

[23] Described by Villon, in *The Testament*, XCV, as a sergeant in the bodyguard of the Provost of Paris. G.P. comments: 'the sergeants of Paris were often no better than those whom they arrested'.

[24] L.T. thinks that this seigneur de Grigny was Philippe Brunel, a bad character who (A.L.) was later on, in 1468, involved in an unsavoury lawsuit. A.L., in annotating the passage referred to, describes Philippe Brunel also as a seigneur de Grigny, but, in another passage, states that the person named by Villon was Etienne Chevalier, who in 1450 was secretary and treasurer to the King.

[25] Both these fortresses were in ruins. (L.T.)

[26] Nothing is known of him. 'Mouton', however, was the false name given by Villon to the barber who dressed his wound after his lethal brawl with the priest Sermoise. Cf. note on XXXIII. (L.T.)

[27] Jacques Raguier, brother of Jean Raguier, mentioned two stanzas earlier, and, like him, a great drinker and glutton. (L.T.) Cf. *The Testament*, XCI.

[28] Officers of the Châtelet prison. (A.L.)

[29] Robert d'Estouteville, Provost of Paris. Villon was received on friendly terms by his wife. (L.T.) Cf. *The Testament*, CXXIX.

[30] Attorney of the community of Saint-Benoît-le-Bientourné (L.T.), where Villon lodged with his foster father.

[31] A journeyman butcher, fined for assault in 1477, and subsequently twice a plaintiff in lawsuits. (L.T.)

[32] Jean du Harley, Captain of the Guard, had the rank of esquire. His right to the office was therefore disputed by a rival, since it was normally reserved for knights. This is why Villon bequeathes to du Harlay 'The Helmet' inn, the words also having the sense of 'knighthood'. (L.T.)

[33] The Three Lilies sculptured or painted on the Châtelet prison. (L.T.)

[34] A sergeant at the Châtelet prison (L.T.) Cf. *The Testament*, LXXXIII and XCVIII. It is not known why Villon disliked him.

[35] Poachers and casual labourers, who later became sergeants at the Châtelet. (L.T.) Cf. *The Testament*, XCIX and C.

[36] Usurer and speculator in salt. (L.T.)

[37] Financier and speculator. (L.T.)

[38] Speculator, engaged in a legal dispute with Robert d'Estouteville. (L.T.)

[39] *Ils mangeront maint bon morceau*, in the original, has the sense of the popular expression: *Ils mangeront les pissenlits par les racines*, 'They'll eat dandelions by the roots.' (L.T.)

[40] Canons of the Church of Saint-Benoît, octogenarians, wealthy, knowing little Latin, quarrelsome and litigious. (L.T.) Cf. *The Testament*, CXXI.

[41] The canons of Saint-Benoît had been reprimanded by the Paris Chapter for failing in their duty to sing at a certain Mass. (L.T.)

[42] Just at this time the canons of Saint-Benoît were taking legal action against the heirs of the butcher Guillot Gueuldry, who for twenty years had been in arrears with the rent he owed on his stall. (L.T.)

[43] A tavern. (L.T.)

[44] The Fifteen Signs of the approach of the Day of Judgment—a common theme for preachers. (L.T.)

[45] A tavern. (L.T.)

[46] The original has an obscene double meaning. (L.T.)

[47] This may refer to a Master of Arts named Jean le Merdi, who eighteen months earlier had disarmed Villon when the latter was engaged in a dagger-brawl with a priest named Philippe Sermoise, who shortly afterwards died of the wounds he had received. Villon received a royal pardon for this homicide. (L.T.)

[48] Erysipelas. (L.T.)

[49] Men of wealth. (L.T.) Merebeuf was a draper, and Louviers was a former alderman. (A.L.)

[50] A ruined village, whose toll yielded Rousseville no income. (L.T.)

[51] A person entrusted by the municipality with the organization of open-air revels on occasions of public rejoicing. (L.T.)

[52] This stanza, and the three following, do not appear in the earliest known edition of Villon's works, published in 1489, nor in the edition by Clément Marot, published in 1533.

NOTES

BALLADE OF THE BLOIS CONTEST

[1] L.T. accepts the tradition that this ballade was written at the court of Charles of Orleans in 1458. (The Duke had composed the first line, and had set his poet-courtiers the competitive task of writing ballades in which this line should be followed by similar paradoxes.) G.P., however, thinks that Villon had already been expelled from the Duke's court, and, hearing of the Contest, sent this poem to the Duke afterwards. The poem is not to be found in the volume, still in existence, in which the Duke copied out poems that had pleased him. (C.M.)

[2] In the original, *Les gages ravoir!* 'let me have my wages again'. Apparently the Duke had granted Villon a stipend, Villon had thereafter fallen out of favour and the stipend had been discontinued.

PETITION TO MY LORD OF BOURBON

[1] Duke John II of Bourbon, whose habitual residence, at Moulins, Villon visited some time about the winter of 1457-58. (L.T. and C.M.)

[2] The Montcorbier family came to Paris from the Bourbonnais. (L.T.)

[3] Mr. Lewis Wharton (*The Poems of François Villon*, J. M. Dent & Sons, Ltd.) has translated this ballade into octosyllabic blank verse, and has translated the refrain as:

> . . . all you will lose
> Will be the time of waiting, sire!

have adapted this translation to my purpose.

[4] L.T. quotes Clement Marot: 'There is no forest around Patay, and no chestnuts are sold there.' Villon's prospective earnings as a gatherer of acorns and chestnuts were therefore poor security for the requested loan.

[5] The cross appearing on certain coins. (L.T.)

THE DEBATE BETWEEN VILLON'S HEART AND HIS BODY

[1] Composed in a dungeon of the prison of Meung. (L.T.)

[2] This planet was supposed to have a baleful and melancholic influence. (L.T.)

[3] Villon attributes this saying to Solomon, not because he believed that Solomon was its author, but because a work popular in the Middle Ages contained a series of dialogues between Solomon and Saturn, in which the latter answers the former's wise remarks with truisms, jests and obscenities. (L.T.)

EPISTLE

[1] Composed, like the immediately preceding poem, in the prison of Meung. (L.T.)

BALLADE FOR FRANCE

[1] The date of this ballade is not known. I have inserted it here because it may well have been written about the time that Villon was set free from the prison of Meung by a royal amnesty. Cf. note 2 to *The Testament*, I.

[2] Mr. Lewis Wharton, op. cit. in note 3 to the 'Petition to my Lord of

NOTES

Bourbon', comments: 'The bittern was supposed to increase its cry by thrusting its beak and head into the water.'

[3] According to a medieval tale, a rich and avaricious Roman emperor named Octavian was executed by his subjects, who melted a gold basin and poured the gold down his throat. (L.T.)

THE TESTAMENT

[1] Some time late in 1461 (cf. stanza XI). *En l'an de mon trentiesme age*, in the original, is poetic licence. In the previous summer Villon had informed the gaol authorities at Meung that he was thirty years old. (G.P.)

[2] Thibault d'Aussigny, bishop of Orleans, who kept Villon in prison at Meung throughout the summer of 1461. Villon was released by Louis XI, in the course of a widespread amnesty to prisoners, granted, as was customary, shortly after the King's accession to the throne. (A.L.)

[3] Jean Cotart, Villon's counsel at the Church court. Cf. CXV and the following Ballade. He died on January 9th, 1461. (L.T.)

[4] The Picards were a heretical sect who believed that prayers should not be spoken aloud. (T.L.)

[5] *Fiant dies ejus pauci, et episcopatum ejus accipiat alter.* (L.T.)

[6] For the reason for this enthusiasm, cf. note to stanza I.

[7] The castle of Moulins, residence of Duke John II of Bourbon. 'Esperance' was the ducal motto. (L.T.)

[8] *Le Romant de la Rose*, a long, allegorical-didactic poem started in 1237 by Guillaume de Lorris and continued in 1280 by Jean de Meung.

[9] Villon is mistaken. The story comes from John of Salisbury's *Policraticus*. (G.P.)

[10] It is not known who he was. G.P. supposes that some of Villon's relatives must have been well-to-do.

[11] A man of enormous wealth and influence whose property was confiscated, and who died in exile in 1456. (L.T.)

[12] A contemporary locution, not necessarily meaning that Villon's father was drowned. (L.T.)

[13] G.P. and L.T. accept the following interesting derivation (hit on by another scholar, M. Ernest Langolis, Professor at the University of Lille), of this odd name: In the Middle Ages, Alcibiades was commonly supposed (e.g. by St. Thomas, in a commentary on Boethius) to have been a woman and to have typified female beauty. Villon's corruption of 'Alcibiade' into 'Archipiada' is explained by the supposition that he had not read the name, but only heard it, at a University lecture or in conversation.

[14] 'Thais' was a generic name for a courtesan. (L.T.)

[15] The well-known translation of *Mais ou sont les neiges d'antan*: 'But where are the snows of yester-year' is by Dante Gabriel Rossetti. I have adopted it, cutting out the superfluous syllable.

[16] G.P. gives the following explanation of the use of the invocation *Prince* as a standard opening to the Envoy of a ballade: 'a quite mechanical survival from the time when Ballades were actually addressed to the "prince" of the Pui (a sort of poetical academy, which awarded prizes for the best ballades)'.

[17] G.P. points out that this title is misleading, since all the persons

mentioned—except Charlemagne, Bertrand Du Guesclin (*d.* 1380) and the Duke of Alençon (who was still alive)—had died quite recently. G.P. gives the following list of names and dates: (*a*) Calixtus III, *d.* 1458. (*b*) Alphonso V, *d.* 1458. (*c*) Charles I, *d.* 1456. (*d*) Artus, *d.* 1458. (*e*) Charles VII, *d.* 1461. (*f*) James II, *d.* 1460. (*g*) John III, *d.* 1458. (*h*) John of Castille, *d.* 1454.

[18] Ladislas, *d.* 1457.

[19] Bertrand Du Guesclin, *d.* 1380.

[20] Berand II, *d.* 1426.

[21] John II. He was condemned to death in 1458, but the sentence was commuted to one of perpetual imprisonment. (G.P. takes this mistake of Villon's as evidence that, when he wrote *The Testament*, he had not returned to Paris from his wanderings.)

[22] I have not attempted to produce an equivalent in more archaic English. In any case, G.P. points out that Villon's way of writing in 'Old French' was simply to substitute *ly* for *le* and to append an *s* to nouns in the singular.

[23] L.T. explains this as meaning 'poor *as* a pedlar of Rennes'. C.M., however, states that this town was the headquarters of the Mercers' Guild, and that the pedlars who sold the mercers' wares had a bad reputation and were generally considered to be affiliated to the *Coquille*, a nationwide secret society of criminals. Villon and his friend Regnier de Montigny were both suspected of being *coquillards*. Cf. note on stanza LXXXVI.

[24] 'The helmet-maker's girl.' The 'belles' of Paris were often shop-girls, and named after the trades at which they worked. (L.T.)

[25] The *Shorter Oxford English Dictionary* quotes Blackstone: 'The king may . . . decry or cry down any coin of the kingdom, and make it no longer current.'

[26] L.T. considers that this Firmin (*Fremin*, in the original, a Picard form of the same name) was an imaginary character. C.M. supposes him to have been a young student who admired Villon's poetry and was proud to do odd jobs for him.

[27] Erysipelas. (L.T.)

[28] The *Decretum Gratiani*, a collection of ecclesiastical judgments published by Gratianus, a monk of Bologna, in 1150, contains a ruling that the guilt of adultery (which, the Decree explains, comprises all extramarital sexual intercourse) is less if it is hidden. (L.T.)

[29] In the original, *Or ont ces fols amans le bont*, a metaphor from tennis. (L.T.)

[30] This and the following stanza are, properly, part of the 'Double Ballade', and in the original have the same rhymes as the four previous stanzas. I have here found it impossible to reconcile the requirements of rhyme with those of translation.

[31] Cf. note on *The Bequests*, III. C.M.'s interpretation of what happened is as follows: Villon had avenged himself for her indifference towards him by composing a defamatory ballade and getting his friends to sing it before her window. Katherine had him arrested for slander and 'blasphemy', and he was whipped in front of her house by the public executioner.

[32] In the original, *Mitaines a ces nopces telles* . . . A reference to a contemporary custom, referred to also by Rabelais, of organizing rough-houses at weddings.

[33] Noël Jolis, mentioned also in *The Testament*, CXLII. A variation of

readings in the original makes it uncertain whether he took part in the beating or was himself also beaten. (L.T.)

[34] Cf., however, stanza LXXXII, in which Villon says that she gave him no encouragement.

[35] Thibault d'Aussigny, Bishop of Orleans (cf. the early stanzas of *The Testament*) is here insultingly called by the name of Tacque Thibault, a onetime favourite of a Duke of Berry, who lavished riches upon him at the public expense, with the result that Tacque Thibault became a name of popular execration. (L.T.)

[36] *Une poire d'angoisse* meant (*a*) a pear of (the village of) Angoisse, (*b*) moral torment, (*c*) a gag for a person undergoing torture. (L.T.)

[37] *Et reliqua*—'and the balance still due'. (L.T.)

[38] A pun on the official's name, Étienne Plaisance. (L.T.)

[39] Petit maistre Robert, so named because, by common practice, he had inherited his office from his father. As executioner he was in charge of the tortures to which Villon was subjected. (L.T.)

[40] Cf. *The Bequests*, XXIII.

[41] Landlord of 'The Pine-Cone'.

[42] Pastrycook.

[43] Vendor of cooked meats. Presumably Villon was in debt to all of them, and they could distrain on his possessions.

[44] Cf. note to stanza XLVII.

[45] Cf. note to stanza XLVII.

[46] *Le Pet au Deable*, 'The Fart against the Devil', was a large stone that stood in a Paris street, whence, in the year 1452, it was carried off by some students into the grounds of the University. The result of this and other similar pranks was that the sergeants of Paris, on orders from the Provost, Robert d'Estouteville, carried out a sort of minor pogrom against all members of the University. (L.T.)

[47] Maître Guy Tabarie, an accomplice of Villon and others in a burglary of the coffers of the college of Navarre, and also, according to his own statement, Villon's accomplice in plotting a burglary from a monk of Angers, a relative of Villon. Cf. *The Bequests*, VI. (A.L.)

[48] A gibe at Tabarie's readiness to give away his accomplices. (L.T.) See Biographical Note.

[49] A pun: Saint Satur is an actual village, and 'satur' also meant 'satyr'. L.T. considers it possible that the village did, in fact, contain the tomb of this legendary lecher, with an epitaph recalling his amorous prowess.

[50] One of the duties of this sergeant of the Châtelet (cf. *The Bequests*, XXIII, and *The Testament*, XCVIII) was to exercise surveillance over prostitutes. (L.T.)

[51] This is how the acrostic runs in the original.

[52] Cf. *The Bequests*, XI.

[53] Cf. *The Bequests*, XI. He had probably refused Villon further help.

[54] Maître Pierre Baubignon. L.T. knows nothing of him except that he was a brother of Jehan Baubignon, canon of Paris and master of appeals.

[55] L.T. has found good reason to suppose that this may have been the sign—namely, a burglar's tool—of the *Coquille*, the society of criminals mentioned in the note on stanza XLII.

[56] Pierre St. Amand, a wealthy financier and a friend of Maître Guillaume de Villon had given the poet employment for his foster-father's sake, but

had reluctantly dismissed him when his wife complained that the young man was nothing but a beggar. (C.M.)

[57] The 'White Horse' and 'Mule' left him in *The Bequests*, XII.

[58] Author of *La Chronique scandaleuse*. (A.L.)

[59] Cf. note to LXVII.

[60] It is not known why Villon calls him *mon avocat*. He was a student contemporary of Villon's in the Faculty of Arts. (A.L.)

[61] Cf. *The Bequests*, XI.

[62] The original contains an obscene and untranslatable pun. *Branc* means both sword and excrement, and *fourreau* means both scabbard and anal orifice. (L.T.)

[63] Cf. *The Bequests*, XIX.

[64] Cf. *The Bequests*, XXXIV.

[65] They were rich bourgeois aspiring to nobility. Nicholas de Louviers was, in fact, ennobled in 1464. (L.T.)

[66] Keeper of a cookshop. (L.T.)

[67] Cf. LXVII and LXXXVIII.

[68] *Le droit d'échevin*, the right to be elected as alderman. (L.T.)

[69] In the original the last two lines of this stanza, and most of the next stanza, are written in Poitevin dialect.

[70] Directions designed to throw the inquisitive off the track. (L.T.)

[71] The twelve sergeants of the Guard. (L.T.)

[72] Jean de Bailly, Parliament attorney and Clerk of Justice to the Treasury. (L.T.)

[73] A public pump. (L.T.)

[74] Cf. note to *The Bequests*, XXXIV.

[75] A sergeant at the Châtelet who took part in the inquiries concerning the robbery from the College of Navarre. (L.T.)

[76] The Company of the Provost's Guard. (L.T.)

[77] Cf. *The Bequests*, XXIII, and *The Testament*, LXXXIII.

[78] Cf. *The Bequests*, XXIV.

[79] Jehan Mahé, nicknamed *l'Orfèvre de bois*, was a sergeant at the Châtelet and an assistant to the Questioner. One of his tasks was to whip naked people. Hence the eroticism of this stanza. (L.T.)

[80] Then believed to be an aphrodisiac. (L.T.)

[81] Merchant furrier and Captain of the Six Score of Paris archers, i.e. police. (L.T.)

[82] A jeer at Riou's police, for whom 'mastiffs' was a slang name.

[83] A reference to Riou's trade.

[84] A rich and avaricious clerk of the Treasury. (L.T.)

[85] Perrot Girard. L.T. conjectures that he added to his earnings as a barber by letting out furnished rooms for immoral purposes. C.M. supposes that he maintained a lodging-house and headquarters for the *Coquille*.

[86] Huguette du Hamel, a notoriously immoral woman, but, in fact, an abbess. (L.T.) Possibly Villon spent some time at Bourg-la-Reine in her company. (C.M.)

[87] Male and female members of a sect that practised what nowadays is called nudism. (L.T.)

[88] Jean de Pouilli, Doctor of Theology and famous preacher, who attacked the Mendicant friars, was rebuked for this by the Pope in 1321, and was compelled to make public retraction. (L.T.)

[89] Jean de Meung, part author of *Le Romaunt de la Rose*.

[90] Author of a *Liber lamentationum Matheoluli*, 1286, translated into French in 1372. (L.T.)

[91] A name deliberately misspelled by Villon. The person referred to may have been Jean Turquan, Lieutenant-Criminal to the Provost. (L.T.)

[92] The place where he kept a mistress. (L.T.)

[93] Richard de la Palu, Sealer to the Bishop of Paris. L.T. supposes that this stanza, which is a gibe at the Sealer's laziness, refers to some action brought against Villon in the Bishop's court, possibly by Katherine de Vausselles. (Cf. notes to the 'Double Ballade' following stanza LIV), or by Denise (cf. *The Testament*, CXV).

[94] Beeswax. (L.T.)

[95] Auditors of the Chamber of Accounts. 'My Lords' is ironical, as they were only subaltern officials. (L.T.)

[96] Macé d'Orléans, lieutenant of the bailiwick of Berry, through which Villon had passed on his wanderings. Villon gives his name a feminine form, as an insult. (L.T., quoting a previous authority, Pierre Champion.)

[97] Maître François de la Vacquerie, prosecutor of the Ecclesiastical Court. (L.T.)

[98] i.e. a rope to hang him. (L.T.)

[99] He must have been assaulted by certain delinquent clerks whom he had prosecuted. (L.T.)

[100] As patron saint of the English, recently occupiers of Paris, he presumably represented, to Villon and his contemporary readers, what is nowadays called 'collaborationism'. The appropriateness, to Villon's mind, of the 'Scots gorget' indicates that the poet did not make any clear distinction between the two nations.

[101] Maître Jean Laurens, another prosecutor of the Ecclesiastical Court. (L.T.)

[102] Archbishop of Bourges and son of the Jacques Cœur mentioned in stanza XXXVI. It is thought that Villon, during his wanderings, made an unsuccessful application to this archbishop for financial help. Cf. *The Testament*, CXXX. (L.T. and C.M.)

[103] Nothing is known of her, or of this case. (L.T.)

[104] This word (from the Greek for 'host') was commonly supposed in the Middle Ages to have been the proper name of the governor of the feast of Cana. (L.T.)

[105] Germain Marle, money-changer. (L.T.)

[106] Cf. *The Bequests*, XXV-XXVI, and notes.

[107] L'ordre des Mathelins, a pun on the word *Mathelin* (or *Mathurin*), which also meant 'fool'. (L.T.)

[108] Maître Pierre Richier, Master in Theology, who was, in fact, a well-known and reputable schoolmaster. (L.T.)

[109] Aelius Donatus, the grammarian, whose book is still used in French schools. (L.T.)

[110] A schoolboys' joke. 'Decus' has the punning significance of 'des culs', so that the last two words mean, in modern English, 'backsides to you!' (L.T.)

[111] Guillaume Cotin and Thibault de Vitri. Cf. *The Bequests*, XXVIII and notes.

[112] The College of the Eighteen Clerks, the oldest College in Paris, and of bad reputation. Scholarships to this college were awarded by the canons

of Notre-Dame, to whose number Guillaume Cotin and Thibault de Vitri themselves belonged. (L.T.)

[113] Michault Culdoe, an alderman of Paris. (L.T.)

[114] Charles Taranne, member of a wealthy Parisian family. (L.T.)

[115] In the fifteenth century such boots had an erotic significance. (L.T.)

[116] Jehanne, a general name for a harlot. (L.T.)

[117] Cf. *The Bequests*, XVIII.

[118] Another ruin. (L.T.)

[119] Jehan de la Garde (cf. *The Bequests*, XXXIII). Thibault and Jehan were both names for a cuckold. (L.T.)

[120] A prosecutor at the Châtelet, and presumably a drinking companion of de la Garde. (L.T.)

[121] Cf. *The Bequests*, XX.

[122] Magistrate at the Châtelet and as such authorized to levy toll on spices. (L.T.)

[123] Another examiner at the Châtelet. (L.T.)

[124] Robert d'Estouteville, former Provost of Paris. (Cf. *The Bequests*, XX.) He had been deprived of office by Louis XI in the summer of 1461. But Villon, who had been in prison at the time, was still unaware of this. (L.T.) G.P. and C.M. infer from this unawareness that Villon cannot have returned to Paris when he wrote *The Testament*.

[125] D'Estouteville won his wife, Ambroise de Loré (whose name appears in an acrostic in the following ballade), at a tournament held by King René of Sicily at Saumur in 1446. (L.T.)

[126] A sneer at d'Estouteville's defeated opponent, Louis de Beauveau, who had translated the *Filostrato* of Boccaccio, which describes the love of Troilus and Cressida. (L.T.)

[127] In 1466 and 1467 Jehan Perdrier was groom and warden of the Royal Palace at Loges, in the forest of St. Germain. (L.T.)

[128] A clerk of finances. (L.T.)

[129] i.e. with the Archbishop of Bourges, Jean Cœur. Nothing is known of this episode. (L.T.)

[130] Chief cook to Charles VI, author of a work entitled *Le Viandier de Guillaume Firel dit Taillevent*. (L.T.)

[131] Maître André Couraud, representative in Paris of King René of Sicily. L.T. supposes that he gave Villon a letter recommending him to the King's court at Angers, on the occasion of Villon's visit to this town. Nothing came of this recommendation.

[132] i.e. the ballade that follows. A certain Philippe de Vitri (*ob.* 1351) had written a poem entitled *Les Dits de Franc-Gontier*, describing the imaginary joys of a sham-pastoral existence. (L.T.)

[133] King René. This monarch had also written a sham-pastoral poem, entitled *Regnault et Jehanneton*, or *les Amours du Berger et de la Bergeronne*. Not daring to attack King René's poem directly, Villon attacks the previous and similar poem. (L.T.)

[134] Cf. preceding note.

[135] Cf. note 132.

[136] C.M. quotes a contemporary recipe for this drink: 'Take half a pound of fine cinnamon; one pound of fine sugar; one ounce of white ginger; one part of cloves, mace and nutmeg; and one part of black pepper—all these spices to be hot and full. Grind them together and add hot wine.'

[137] De Vitri had expatiated on the delights of listening to birdsong. (L.T.)

[138] Mademoiselle de Bruières, widow of a notary who was secretary to Charles VI and proprietor of the 'House of the Pet-au-Deable', so-called because the stone mentioned in LXXVIII stood in front of it. She had presumably complained to the civil authorities when the students removed this stone, and had therefore been partly responsible for the ensuing persecution. (L.T.)

[139] Perhaps because the public cemeteries of Paris were also used by prostitutes in search of custom; perhaps because they were also used as places for the delivery of regular religious sermons. (L.T.)

[140] The women of the Halles (public markets) were noted for their readiness of tongue. (L.T.)

[141] The Abbey of Montmartre, whose nuns were notorious for the laxity with which they admitted men to the premises. (L.T.)

[142] Upon this hill stood a hermitage and a small chapel served by monks. (L.T.)

[143] *La Grosse Margot.* As A.L. points out, this is the name of a tavern—the tavern, in fact, at whose door Regnier de Montigny was arrested for assaulting the police. (Cf. note to *The Bequests*, XVIII)—and *not* as used to be commonly supposed, the name of a harlot.

[144] Cf. note to immediately preceding stanza.

[145] 'Go, go!' in the original—an expression presumably dating from the English occupation of Paris.

[146] *J'ay mon pain cuit*, in the original, means: 'I have finished my life of pleasure and have an assured livelihood.' (L.T.)

[147] In the original the first six lines of this envoy contain an acrostic, their initial letters spelling 'Villon'.

[148] Noël Jolis. Cf. the reference to him in the 'Double Ballade' following stanza LIV.

[149] Maître Henri Cousin, master executioner of Paris. (L.T.)

[150] In the original, *les perdus*, meaning both 'lost children' and 'lost souls', or criminals.

[151] Criminals frequently lodged in brothels. (L.T.)

[152] In the original, *Se vouls ales a Montpipeau*: from *piper*, to swindle; *ou a Ruel*, from *ruer*, to knock down and rob: phrases of the Cant. (L.T.) Montpipeau was, however, also the name of the place where Colin de Cayeulx was hanged. (C.M.)

[153] i.e. an appeal from the secular authority to the Church Court.

[154] A delinquent cleric and childhood friend of Villon. He was hanged, as an incorrigible rogue, in 1460. (L.T.)

[155] Forged indulgences.

[156] Perjurers were boiled alive. (L.T.) In 1455 ten members of the Coquille were boiled in oil at Dijon. (C.M.)

[157] Clowning beggars and tricksters wore motley garb. (L.T.)

[158] An asylum for the blind. (L.T.)

[159] The Cemetery of the Innocents, where the blind were allowed to solicit alms and to earn money by mourning for the dead. (L.T.)

[160] This saint was wrongly believed to have founded the Inquisition. The Inquisitors were entitled to try people for heresy even after their deaths. (L.T.)

[161] Cf. *The Bequests*, XVI.

[162] A pastoral ditty.

[163] Maître Pierre Lomer, a canon of Notre-Dame, had recently been instructed by the Chapter to evict a number of harlots from their lodgings. (L.T.)

[164] A legendary knight who saved maidens from rape. (L.T.)

[165] Alain Chartier had also addressed the love-sick. (L.T.)

[166] Proprietor of a public hot-air bath frequented mostly by loose women. (L.T.)

[167] The original contains an untranslatable joke. James had recently inherited a building on the *rue aux Truyes*, the Street of Sows. Villon gives warning to any woman who might consider marrying James, that he will leave his property to his present family. (L.T.)

[168] Pierre de Brèze, Grand Seneschal of Normandy, who had recently been imprisoned by Louis XI. He was an enemy of Villon's patron, Robert d'Estouteville (cf. *The Bequests*, XX, and *The Testament*, CXXVIII et seq.) It seems, therefore, that to please his patron, and not knowing that the latter, too, was in prison, the poet was jeering at a man who had shown him kindness. (L.T.)

[169] Mareschal means both 'Marshal' (either Field-Marshal or sergeant, etc.) and also 'farrier'. (L.T.)

[170] The pages of the Captain of the Guard, and of officers of the Crown generally, were notorious for their effrontery and turbulence. (L.T.)

[171] Villon therefore assigns to the Captain two bad characters whom the Chief of Military Police, Tristan l'Hermite, had recently dismissed from service. (L.T.)

[172] Jean Chappelain, a sergeant of the Twelve at the Châtelet prison; mentioned here, presumably, only for the sake of a pun. (L.T.)

[173] Villon was theoretically entitled to a junior benefice, but was in no likelihood of ever receiving one. (L.T.)

[174] Jehan of Calais, notary at the Châtelet. (L.T.)

[175] Receiver of stolen goods.

[176] The Chapel of Saint-Avoye was on a first floor, so that no dead could be buried there. (L.T.)

[177] Cf. note to CLXIII.

[178] Cf. note 153 to first stanza following CXLV. Villon had apparently also tried on some occasion to profit by his right of appeal to the Church Court. This appeal of his is to be distinguished from his Appeal to Parliament made in the winter of 1462-63 (cf. the ballade entitled 'Question asked of the Gaol-Clerk').

[179] Jacqueline, the great bell of Notre-Dame, cracked on several occasions and in 1451 was recast. (L.T.)

[180] 'Loaves of St. Stephen' was a popular expression meaning the stones with which the Saint was lapidated. (L.T.)

[181] A rich merchant and speculator in salt. (L.T.)

[182] The grocer mentioned also in *The Bequests*, XXXIII, and *The Testament*, CXXXVII.

[183] Lieutenant-Criminal to the Provost of Paris. (L.T.)

[184] President of the Chamber of Judicial Enquiries. (L.T.)

[185] Cupbearer to Louis XI. (L.T.)

[186] For Brunel, cf. *The Bequests*, XVIII, and *The Testament*, CXXVI. For Raguier, cf. *The Bequests*, XIX, and *The Testament*, XCI. For James, cf. *The Testament*, CLVI. All three were poor and disreputable.

[187] *Le Maistre des Testaments* was an ecclesiastical official whose right to settle disputes concerning wills was denied by Parliament. (L.T.)

[188] A young priest who took his University degree in arts in 1452, at the same time as Villon. (L.T.)

[189] *Jouer à ung tripot*, in the original, means both 'to play tennis' and 'to enjoy the sport of love'. (L.T.)

[190] A contemporary bawdy song. (L.T.)

[191] A leading wine-merchant. (L.T.)

[192] *Dures crottes*, in the original. These 'harsh crusts' were probably the gags that were thrust into the mouths of prisoners undergoing torture.

[193] Medieval Latin for a quaternary of bells.

[194] His body. (Partridge's *Dictionary of Slang*.)

VILLON'S EPITAPH

[1] L.T. assigns no date to this poem. C.M. seems to suggest that it was written in the prison of Meung in 1460. G.P. says that it was written in the Châtelet prison at Paris late in 1462. If this is so, for the circumstances in which the poem was written, cf. note 1 to the ballade: 'Question asked of the gaol clerk'.

JE SUIS FRANÇOIS...

[1] In the original this poem is four lines long. I have found it impossible to render its meaning (e.g. the joke: 'Je suis François . . .) in so short a space.

[2] This joke (of indicating Paris's geographical situation by reference to a small town) may have been enriched by the fact that Pontoise acquired fame when it was regained by Charles VII after an important victory in September 1441. (L.T.)

[3] Villon was three times under sentence of death—at Orleans in the summer of 1460, at Meung in the summer of 1461, and at Paris in the winter of 1462-63. (C.M.) L.T. considers that this poem was written on the third of these occasions.

QUESTION ASKED OF THE GAOL-CLERK

[1] In November 1462 Villon was arrested by the police after a brawl at which, so far as is known, he was merely a bystander. Since he was in very bad odour with the authorities, both civil and ecclesiastical, the Provost's Court took the opportunity to condemn him to be hanged and strangled. Villon appealed to Parliament, which commuted the sentence to one of ten years' banishment from Paris. (L.T. and C.M.)

[2] Étienne Garnier, gaol clerk at the Châtelet, presumably tried to dissuade Villon from making this appeal. (L.T.)

[3] Hugues Capel, King of France, 987-996, and founder of the Third Dynasty, was popularly supposed to have been related to a family of butchers. (L.T)

[4] Villon was put to the Question under torture by water, and was presumably forced to confess to crimes of which he was innocent. (C.M.)

[5] In the original, *escorcherie*, 'a flaying-place', i.e. a place of torture. (L.T.)

[6] In the original, *joncherie*, a Cant word equivalent to the modern 'line of talk' or 'spiel'. The implied taunt is that Garnier ('a very suspect person'—L.T.) would naturally understand Cant.

IN PRAISE OF THE COURT

[1] Addressed to Parliament in the circumstances explained in note 1 to the immediately preceding ballade. The real purpose of the poem is made clear in the envoy. It is not known whether Villon was given the three days' grace he asked for.